The Rideshare Chronicles

Destination Destiny

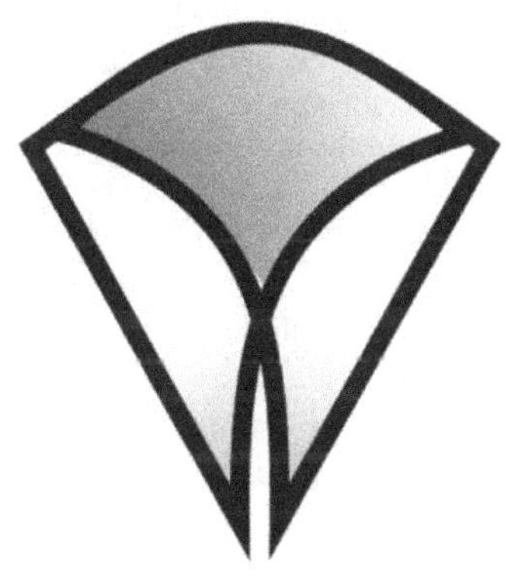

Frieda Josephine Lopez

Publisher: Absolute Author Publishing House
Editor: Dr. Melissa Caudle
Associate Editor: Kathy Rabb Kittok
Cover Designer: Rebeca @rebecacovers

Paperback ISBN: 978-1-64953-069-1
eBook ISBN: 978-1-64953-070-7

Dedication

I dedicate this book to all the essential workers who have put their lives at risk during this most pressing time. It's because of you, Americans, that the world is great. To all my dreamers, always remember never to give up and always have faith in yourself. It's your time to shine next. To my late Uncle Miguel Lopez, you finally were put in an epic story. Thanks for teaching me the lessons you taught throughout my life. Semper Fi. To my late Abuela Juanita Campos, I finally became the warrior woman you always wanted me to be. Te Quiero and extrano mucho. To Mi Gente in San Antonio and Houston, always stay vigilant and strong. Let them hear our voices. To all my sisters worldwide, remember you were always a heroine to my dad. Thank you for the love and support you give us kids daily to all the single dads and men raising children. You're the real MVP.

And a special dedication to my amazing and beloved friend Eddie Sepulveda. RIP my amazing, loved friend. Thank you for sparking something I never thought I ever would gain—the joy of life, love, and the freedom of expression. Your fighting spirit will always and forever be in my heart and my soul.

“When all bets are off, and the only thing you’re fighting for is yourself, build the courage to fight. Because you matter, win or lose, and when you don’t beat yourself up, you gained something you never once had. You gained courage.”

Frieda Lopez

TABLE OF CONTENTS

Chapter 1

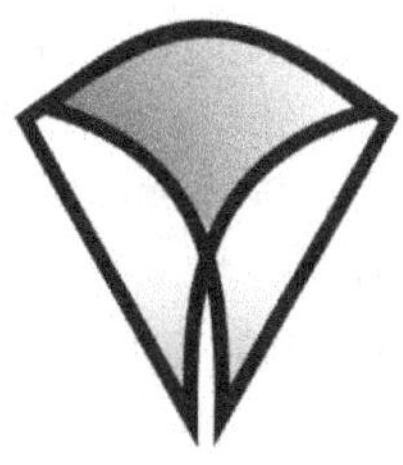

She could feel the hot, oppressive air hit her face in the orange glow of the most traumatic moment of her life. She gasped for air, and for a moment, stunned in the image of the rising shadow that overpowered her intimidating figure. She paused for a minute before the Enchanted Rock to see where she could turn in the maze that it was. Could she turn and swim across the murky water that stood between her and freedom, or should she go into the ocean of paths in the maze of boulders in the deserted park? For the first time in her life, she felt that this might be the end of her life.

"I can't swim fast enough to escape," she told herself in paralyzed fright.

She heard the gaping sound of the screech behind her, and she continued to go down the maze of paths. For the first time, she regretted that she didn't work out as her uncle told her back when she was seventeen.

You need to stay fit if you're going to take this MMA stuff seriously, she could hear him say in her head.

I know Uncle Mike, she condescendingly said in her head like she always did. "Maybe today is the day I meet our Maker and join you on the other side," she said jokingly, which was her usual way of dealing with traumatic events.

She heard the crunching of the leaves getting closer. It crunched like potato chips as it got closer and closer, and then it paused. She also heard the campers' screaming. She attempted to warn them as she ran past the foolish and cliche couple. The screams and a plea for their life and then a pop continued to drift her way. The pop sounded like the popping of her favorite hood rat snack, her Flaming Hot Cheetos.

Fuck! That bastard found those naïve hipster campers. Fucken idiots, she told herself in the conversation in her head.

Alessandra, idiots are fucken idiots! You can't save everyone! Uncle Mike scolded in her head.

"You always told me not to have tolerance or pity idiots," she reassured herself as she continued down the bending path that was trail number three.

"You're regretting taking that cardio regimen serious now, huh Miss Know It All. It would've helped you in swimming that river like you were swimming the Rio Grande," Uncle Mike said in that joking way like he did when he was alive.

"If you're going play Morgan Freeman Tio and be a little more motivating unless you want to see your favorite niece become a psycho's fucken pin cushion," she said in a resentful and dismissive tone.

"Sorry, Mija," the voice repeated empathetically.

The trail was as unfamiliar as running down the path revealed in portions at first and collectively a field maze of petrified trees. Going down the path, it became darker as the glow of the orange night sky revealed further down the trail as the smokey and dense arid fog surrounded her clique San Antonian's body.

"Leave it to this dumb bitch to pick the typical path like the clique horror movie chick that gets killed," she said in her this is it tone. "Damn, I should have had kids!"

"Idiot," Uncle Mike's voice said as he mimicked Napoleon Dynamite.

"Uncle Mike, really!" she said out loud in anger.

"Stay focused, bitch. Remember the story I told you about when I was in the Marine Corps. Face the fear and don't lose focus. You're down this road for a reason," he reassured her.

She focused and ran toward the boulder that she would always see and called the "Mountain Peak." The boulder was one that she had always wanted to climb but felt she didn't have the upper body strength.

"I could be a pin cushion for Mr. Stabby, or I can climb this boulder," she said in her Dr. Phil impression.

"Start climbing bitch; he's three yards away!" Uncle Mike said in alarm.

She attempted the first time and couldn't get past the first three feet as she slipped down the rocks; her arm gave out in trying to lift herself past the fourth foot of the boulder. The second attempt didn't get her past the first foot of the boulder. She fearly looked back. He was one yard away.

She wept as she mumbled to herself in defeat, "I'm dying today.

"Alessandra, why are you quitting, you stupid bitch! Climb! Use that adrenaline and start climbing as your life depended on it. Because it kind of now does," Uncle Mike's voice said.

She looked back. Three hundred meters! She focused and started climbing. She heard the clinking of the blade he used as he tried to stab her leg. The blade was two centimeters from penetrating her leg, which she felt the velocity of the blade as she lifted it past the first six feet off the boulder. She continued to climb as Mr. Stabby slipped down the boulder. She climbed faster and faster. Not realizing it, she was thirty-five feet off the ground as she looked down at Mr. Stabby.

He was tall, dark, and handsome. He had that enchanting five o'clock shadow that your typical British villain had with shaggy dark brown hair. He typically was Alessandra's wet dream until he tried to murder a bitch. He was six foot two inches and chiseled like a Greek god. He dressed in black cargo pants with a black distressed leather jacket that crossed the question, "Did he get that at Marshall's?" His complexion tanned to a golden caramel, and his chiseled face in the normal world would have probably gotten him a modeling contract. Of course, Alessandra, being raised by men and a feminist duo of abuelas, was prone to crotch watching every so often. Since he was her cliche wet dream, she noticed before the attempted murderous attack that he was packing more than she perceived as he slipped the first few feet off the boulder.

"I guess the looks made up for the lack of brain cells, cocksucker," she said mockingly.

"Don't get cocky, girl," Uncle Mike smirked.

"I guess you didn't realize that your jacket concealed armory, and it is what's holding you down, pendejeo," she said confidently.

He looked on the sides of the open jacket and took it off, revealing his chiseled biceps and the marking of the organization against which she was fighting. He took off the holsters that held the machete, the bow, arrows, and the diverse knife collection she didn't realize he had. He inserted his weapons of choice in a holster strapped to his thigh and holstered the harpoon-like bow and arrow gun quicker than a single woman heading to Walgreens for plan B after a one-night stand and started climbing

"Oh, shit!" she said in a terrifying scream.

"See, I told you, pendeja," Uncle Mike said, scolding and followed with "start climbing cause your life depends on it now.

She climbed faster and with agility. She heard him getting to the first peek of the boulder; she was closer to the top. As she rose, there was a problem. To get to the ultimate peak, the only thing stopping her from getting to it was the lack of equipment, as a thick vined rock plant was the only way to get her to the top.

"You want my ass dead, don't you, God?" she yelled in anger as she looked up at the cloudy, half orange glowing sky.

"Remember the weight distribution rules," Uncle Mike reassured her in her head.

"I'm a gordita Uncle Mike; that bitch won't hold my ass," she said sarcastically.

"It's like the men you date, use the one-minute man technique," he said affirmingly.

"My ass is going to fall to my death," she said desperately.

"Have faith, my girl. The odds have always been in your favor," he confirmed.

She looked up at the rooted branch, and she reached up as she lifted herself, raised her body, and grabbed the branch rooted out the boulder.

"I did it," she said proudly. "I fucken did it," she screamed.

Mr. Stabby was on the peak to climb up. He attempted to use the blade he packed and slipped as the titanium blade snapped into the rock. He looked for other ways of getting on the rock, which had no other way up than climbing equipment.

Alessandra looked down as she pulled out her cellphone to call 911. In the park, this was the only way to attain cellphone service. She called 9-1-1 - a busy signal.

"Great, this is the fucken apocalypse," she said.

"Might be," Uncle Mike said. "At least you're safe from that cocksucker."

"No fucken kidding," she repeated back.

She heard a shriek coming down from ten feet below her as her face turned frightened. She saw Mr. Stabby tear off his black wifebeater and saw what looked like scaled spikes form on his back. They grew larger and larger every second. His body disengaged in the bloody mess that was his vessel and revealed his true form. He was a demonized serpent that grew from a six-foot man to a forty-foot dragon at Alessandra's eye level.

The beast was black and spotted with hairy, dark brown spots that resembled warts. It had patches of fluffy hair that looked like the 90s pen she used from *Clueless* inspired as a high school student. His teeth were jagged and looked like a hunting knife unit, the cheap ones found at the Dollar Store. Its yellow eyes had a glowing green iris, something that you would see if the Predator and the Aliens reproduced. The serpent's skin was scaley and dry, like the clay roads she would drive through in El Paso, Texas, at her previous job.

"I wasn't expecting that," Uncle Mike's voice said shockingly.

"You always said the bigger they are, the harder they fall," Alessandra said as she reached for the rock and aimed it right for the eye of the beast.

The beast shrieked in agonizing pain as she impaled the tock deep into the eye, releasing oozing black blood as one eye protruded out.

"Not today Satan, you fucked with the wrong bitch," she said as she aimed for the second one.

The beast let out another agonizing screech as she threw several more rocks until she heard the popping that sounded like the first kernel of a microwave popcorn bag.

"I didn't teach you that one, Mija," Uncle Mike's voice said.

"Game Theory at the basic level; always aim for the eye of every humongous beast. It worked for Lara Croft; it had to work for me," she reassured.

"Now what you deformed, *Never-Ending Story* reject?" she screamed. "You think this shit was going to scare me, huh?" she yelled again. "I hope you know I was always the weird kid and low key. I felt this was going to one day happen, but never exactly like this, you cocky fuck," she said insultingly.

She aimed between its eyes, which biology and anatomy always said is where every endoskeleton living being would have. She missed it by three inches as the beast cocked his head back, vibrating its body like it was about to go into convulsions.

"What's happening," she asked Uncle Mike, unsure.

"I don't know, cabrona, you're the fucken expert," he said derisively. It revealed itself when Uncle Mike said in a panic, "Jump!"

The beast ejected two other heads from its neck's left and right sides.

Alessandra ran to the opposite side of the cliff and looked down at the potential areas she could land. The only thing she found was a bundled bunch of what looked like the only live trees in the area.

"Are you crazy, Uncle Mike?" she said in a frenzied tone.

"When I was in the military," he said as Alessandra interrupted.

"This is not a time for one of your tall tales," she said firmly.

"The odds are in your favor," he said.

As she was about to jump, she felt this stagnant spritz of humid air behind her. She immediately ran and jumped.

As she jumped, rushing down the cliff, she saw the beast dart down as it followed her with faster velocity. As she closed her eyes, she heard the clicking of its jaws opening and ended up feeling the breath of the beast; she opened her eyes to look at the life around her and saw teeth coming closer to her. What was soon to be a dead body that ended as a snack for a *Never-Ending Story* reject of a dragon excuse.

Chapter 2

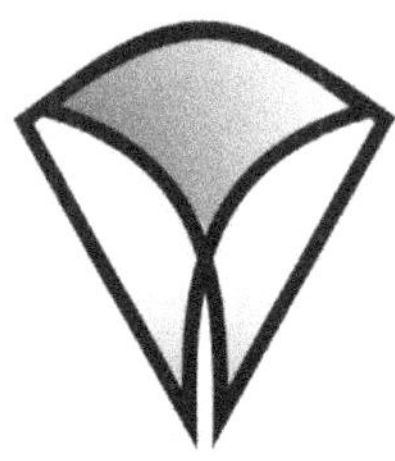

It was 12:15 a,m, when she ejected up from her full-size bed in the room; she lived the thirty-four years of her life in her childhood home in what was the West Side of San Antonio, Texas that July evening. The beads of sweat glistened in the glow of the lights of her neighbors' porch where her best friend Jacob and his mom lived. They lived adjacent to the right of her humble now considered the North West Side neighborhood, which bared the boogie name Memorial Heights upon her return from living in Houston for the last three years. Jacob was working on something as usual as she heard the shuffling of hardware he collected throughout the years after he moved back home five years ago.

"Why the fuck am I having the continuation of this fucken dream," she whispered to herself.

Alessandra was trying to recall the previous dreams she used to have as a child repeated sporadically after her uncle, Godfather, and beloved Uncle Mike died about fourteen years ago. She was staring into the darkness, trying to remember the bits and pieces she could recall. The only thing remembered was of her favorite climbing park, Enchanted Rock. She was wearing one of the few things she could salvage in the demise of her life she used to live in Houston, which ended in a very traumatic way. She wore this French satin shorty set that her client gifted during her independent contract gig for doing an unorthodox position she had, which he adored and worshipped her for. She was five feet and eleven inches and stockier than most girls and had caramel colored skin that was smoother than the satin she wore. She had golden-brown eyes that glistened a hazel honey color in the darkness's light she found comforting. She had strong facial features that resembled more Creole than her Brazilian, Mexican, Puerto Rican, and Cuban background that made her appear more exotic, as people couldn't tell if she was Arabic or a Spaniard. Her thick dark hair faded into a coffee caramel color that she wore in a bun to keep the natural wave intact. She always hated sweating as she felt dirty every time, but in the artificial light, she perceived what everyone at the gym would complement her on back home in Houston. She glowed a Greek goddess, which she hated as she felt it was a cheap way of hitting on her.

The life she brought back was still in bags and boxes from her move three months ago. You could always count on her to have the essentials she always carried, hoping to reach her childhood dreams in the city she deemed the

New York City of Texas, her sketchpad, her pen/pencil pouch, her journal, and her Book of Dreams. She secretly obsessed over the metaphysical world, which became a childhood obsession after all the many unexplained things she experienced.

It reminded her of her early years, desperately like everyone trying to make sense of the madness in a burning world. She was good at recalling many things, but the dreams she had not so much. It secretly scared her that she analyzed her dreams to the unresolved traumatic issues she had throughout her life. She didn't resolve the ones before leaving what she referred to as the "shithole," which was just resentment of the things she didn't understand, after moving to a city living a fast-paced lifestyle she adored, and even harder to understand. She read the passage that she wrote three months after moving from San Antonio that read:

> *I miss San Antonio, TX, so much because I feel like I left behind the life I secretly took for granted, which was my family and the small group of lifelong friends that remained in my life even after high school. Some days, I feel scared as there is way more crime reported here. Before writing this journal entry, I told Scott, my roommate, that "we live in the Galleria, and this shit still happens." Most of the crime was from gang rivalries and stayed away from the boogie area of Alamo Heights because it's not gated, unlike the Dominion. He said that I have to keep an eye out and not provoke anything, and I will be okay. But he knows me well enough to know I*

don't know when to shut up. My ass is going to die in Houston, TX, eventually.

The one thing that I will say is that life is always busy, so I don't have time to worry about this too much. I felt in San Antonio, TX. I had too much time on my hands as I got caught up in the usual social norm there, which basically was work, eat, and drink the pain away, feeling like this was it for me, where moving to Houston has me having a new definition of hope. Not because I have more opportunities, but I am engaged in the hustle and bustle of Houston's social norms. I am tired of hustling; I am active now, cycling and enjoying Houston, TX's wonderful greenery. It's humid as fuck, but it randomly rains. After that spontaneous shower, the breeze that follows is like nature giving me natural air conditioning. Here, I am exposed to new music, but don't mess with a good thing. I stayed true to Journey.

My Uncle Mike always talked about his time when he served in the USMC. He always listened to Journey's "Lights," which I naturally played while I was sitting at the boardwalk in Galveston, TX, which I visited yesterday after training with another store manager in a nearby city. I cried and thought of him. He always talked about being stationed in San Francisco, California, which always brought a tear to his eye. It made me miss him so much. I think this is the feeling he was talking about when he spoke of the lights that go down by the city. I miss home, but I feel like this *is where I am meant to be. I miss home like crazy. I tell Abuela that the crime is a scare tactic used to get me to run back home. My Uncle Mike always said, "I left San Antonio, TX," as he always would tell me, you're going to get trapped here forever.\ All women in San Antonio seem to get married and become a slave to a man, as he always said we were a slave to the man already. I wonder if he's looking down at me just to check in and make sure I am okay. I hope he's proud. I hope I always make him proud. And yes, I finally admitted I was an emotional person and a crier since Scott calls me out on it. Asshole. This is how it feels to make a mark in the world, I finally realized.*

"What a fucken idiotic dreamer," she said repulsively. She picked up her dilapidated iPhone XS, which was full of notifications from Passeio. Passeio was the new rideshare company that began its test run in San Antonio, TX.

"Make extra money this weekend. Do five consecutive rides back-to-back and get a $20.00 bonus until 2:00 AM," it read.

"Hey, if I am going to deal with the shitty attitude of my gender and misperception that rideshare drivers are transporters and not chauffeurs, I can tolerate a few of these 'Keeping up with Kardashians when a bitch should keep up with their damn bills' kind of bitch," she said insultingly. After she checked all the non-essential messages that were spam and the pendejos of her past desire to date again, she realized it was 12:50 a.m.

"Holy shit, I need to get on it if I want to pay this almost suspended cellphone. I kind of need to do this fucken job," she said sarcastically to herself.

She jumped out of bed and saw her angelic abuela sitting watching *Telemundo* with her great aunt, who lived with them in the 840-square foot home that housed her disabled father.

"Good Morning, Princess," she said in her normal nurturing tone. "Are you hungry? I made you a plate, your favorite Arroz con gandules," she added.

"No, Abuela, I'm already running late. I'm going to shower and change and embrace my inner Llorona," she recited back.

"Okay, Mija, I figured, so I put a twenty-dollar bill in your middle console so you can pick up some dinner," she politely replied.

"Abuela, you're barely making it with this bullshit social security check; you don't have to do that," she rebutted.

"We always make it, Mija, and what did I tell you about that mouth," Tia Aurora replied.

"Yes, ma'am, I am sorry," she replied shamefully.

"Hermana, leave her alone, she's a big city girl now, but yes Mija ease up on the malicetes," she said in a caring tone that turned stern.

"Yes, ma'am, I will, and thank you. You know I have all this marked down on how much I owe you already. Did Daddy eat at least," she asked.

"Yes, he did. Don't you worry about us. Go kick ass and rule the road," she replied confidently.

"Thank you, Abuela, and thank you, Tia. You guys are truly a blessing. I know I'm a burden, but I appreciate everything you have done for me since I've returned from Houston. I can't thank you enough," she replied thankfully.

"We are a small family, but we always have each other's back. We never let those who suffer go without. You know that, and I am proud of what you did in Houston. I know I will never replace your mother, but you made me a proud mommy," Abuela said appreciatively.

"Thank you, Abuela. You'll always be my mom," she reassured lovingly.

Chapter 3

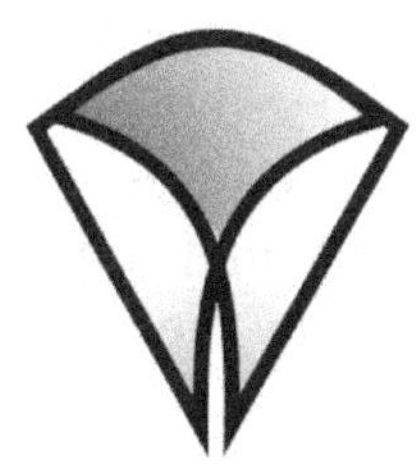

It was 1:15 a.m. Saturday when Alessandra finally hit the road, which was still evening for the nightlife of San Antonio. While driving down Culebra Rd, hitting the I-10, merging onto the ramp, she saw a sight that brought her joy after washing the junkyard that was the interior of the Nissan Silver Rogue she rented to drive for Passeio. The lit-up skyline was her hometown of San Antonio. When she hit the 281 Freeway, a tear fell from her eye. Her eyes glistened in the stary early morning sky, the Hemisphere Tower. She pulled over on the highway's median, flashed her hazards, and got off the utility vehicle to take a picture that had her face to face with the remarkable architecture of the rotating tower.

"I can't believe I resented this remarkable city," she said now in tears.

She turned the opposite direction, ran across the deserted highway of 281, and gazed at the Alamodome. She had so many happy memories there. The day she saw Selena and became star struck. The first time she became a die-hard fan of the San Antonio Spurs, even with their losing streak. The highlight of her entire life that made her want a pony was when she first stepped on the rodeo grounds and got to ride on a horse that showed a bonding love from the first moment she met him. And the way the horse's owner said, "He only does that with special people," which she remembered when she was four years old. The high school random skip a day that she and her misfits' band took when Fiesta entailed a full-fledged carnival. She continued to stare at the other remarkable architecture and kneeled while breaking down in tears.

She couldn't help but scream in joyful tears and excitedly, "I'm back fucken home bitches.

The whistling sound of fireworks metaphorically sounded seconds after she screamed as if it was a rehearsed part of a movie. She watched the glimmering glittering lights, followed by illegal fireworks, which, coincidently, the city's Southwest side residents ignited. She observed a spray of different colored lights that ignited, probably with leftover supply they had in storage from the most recent holiday. She smiled to herself as she crossed the two-car traffic lane that she would pick up after the last call.

"It's a fucken sign bitch" she whispered to herself.

She realized that she missed four ride requests in her brief moment, which she didn't care about at the moment. It just wasn't meant to be. The feeling she had was one of the best feelings she felt in a long time. It was comforting.

It was real. She thought to herself while she sat at the emergency median of 281, between the Commerce exit and the Hemisphere Park exit, and thought about all the good times she has had. She could relive every moment like it was yesterday. Ironically, the memory of her first attempt to drive the highway when she "borrowed" her dad's car when they lived at the Broadview Apartments and joyrode with her two best friends during her teenage years. *AR Jay Martinez and Christina Trevino*. She broke down and cried again.

"I miss them so much; she said reminiscently.

AR Jay and Christina were her ride and die. Her childhood friends were incredibly special to her. But AR Jay and Christina saved her life one homecoming night when they beat the crap out of the high school heartthrob everyone wooed about thinking he's a swell and good guy. I mean, they saved not only her virginity; they saved her sanity, helping her patiently, always making sure she went out and grieved the traumatic situation which didn't stop there.

During the second traumatic situation, they visited her when her ex-husband brutally assaulted her the second time at their favorite club. They came to her rescue when Officer Matthews called them when she lived in Balcones Heights when she fought back and beat herself for almost beating her now ex-husband, now eleven years in her act of self-defense. They always showed up. For her Uncle Mike's funeral, her Abuela J's funeral and never left her side, making a point always to have a slumber party to make sure their beloved friend didn't pop a gasket and go on a crazy streak.

"How would I survive the fuckery of life specifically without those two?" she told herself, while the Jennifer Lopez Album "On the 6" was playing, which now played their iconic song "Waiting for Tonight." It made her cry even more.

She remembered the falling out she had a year before moving to Houston that resulted in a denial of enabled behavior they feared was potentially turning into an addiction. The night that they had the falling out, she recalled her dancing on tables and acting like an idiot when she was using it as an emotional crutch for the previous rape she experienced, that of which she was still in denial. It was because of that confrontation she told them they were dead to her. It was that night that she told them she hated them. It was that moment when she said, "You're jealous of me," that had them walk away. What followed was horrible, "You never will exist to me, and I will never talk to you even in life." That broke her heart. She had no reason to be mad. It was the truth.

She saw red and blue lights circling behind her and saw that the SAPD came to see what was going on in the middle of the night.

"Is everything okay, ma'am?" the officer asked Alessandra. "Can I get your license and registration, please, ma'am?" He asked in a charming and pleasant tone.

The officer was young and attractive, with dark brown eyes and a naturally tanned complexion. He was clean-cut and had little facial hair, with full and kissable lips. He was five-foot eight-inches and very fit, with his biceps popping out of his creased sleeve like a stray hair.

"Yes, Officer Martinez, everything is fine," she said politely.

"I saw that you were kneeling on the side of the road taking pictures of the Alamo," he replied in a comforting tone. "I wanted to make sure you were emotionally okay," he said kindly.

"Yeah, I was taking in the scenery," she replied humbly.

"The city is beautiful, isn't it," he replied proudly. "Are you not from here?" he asked inquisitively.

"Born and raised, but I moved back about three months ago, but today driving for Passeio made me appreciate it for what it's truly worth," she replied in the same reminiscent voice she felt.

"They say it's a city with a small-town feel, which if you ask me is the charming part of San Antonio," he replied like a narrator on the History Channel in his deep sultry voice.

"You know it is; I had a resentment for my hometown for the longest; they always undermined me in Houston as we are that," she said in an assuring tone. "But the truth of the matter is that San Antonio gets underestimated. People don't realize the power and the strength this city has. Despite all the contradictions, tonight I realized that I wasn't appreciative of the things I had here," she said humbly.

It was 1:45 a. m. when the requests started coming in as they heard the Passeio mobile app's whimsical alert.

"Well, Miss Romero, I won't hold you up any longer as you do more for this city than you know being a rideshare driver. Since Passeio, our drunk driver rate has gone down. Thank you for your services, ma'am. We always get thanked for our services, but we rarely thank our rideshare drivers. If no one has told you yet, thank you for the service you provide to this city daily, and welcome home, Miss Alessandra. It's a pleasure to have you back home. Be careful out there," he said in a thankful and appreciative tone.

"Thank you, Officer Martinez, and be safe out there too. If I am in a jam, I might need a kind and amazing soul like you," she replied.

"Call me Alejandro, all my friends do. Have a great rest of your day, Alessandra," he said as he got into the squad car.

While she glanced at the phone to accept the app's ride request, she looked up and saw Officer Alejandro Martinez wave. She waved back and couldn't get over the feeling she was feeling. She took the emergency lights off and said, "It's great to be back home."

Chapter 4

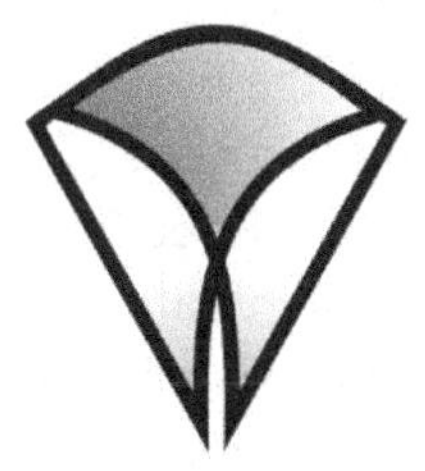

The night didn't go as Alessandra expected. During one of the most challenging times, she had to endure a short-lived career in the adult film industry, embarrassing since people perceive these women as being degraded. Today she realized how degrading it could be. During the most challenging times, she embarked on a fun and satisfying career, literally speaking. But it was a delight as she did this with the one and only Jonathan King, one of the top trending stars in the industry. She made friends with him one drunken college night while partying with her sorority. Jonathan Knight and she met one drunken night that would have ended traumatically if he didn't intervene.

Jonathan King was six feet four inches back in college with a baby face and a café con leche complexion, which made a golden tan on a gringo mixed with Italian. He had a faux hawk that shagged at the very top then, which she would joke about him being a hipster with his impeccable taste of style. He had broad shoulders and muscular arms that matched his muscular calves. His lips were pinkish nude, and he had a chiseled face that reminded her of Jason Boreanaz back in his *Buffy the Vampire Slayer* days. What started as a friendship turned into an intense romance that ended up in heartbreak. Not the cliche girl meets boy; boy breaks her heart. But the boy meets the girl, and the girl breaks the boy's heart scenario. It wasn't because she was a cold-hearted bitch; it was because of the unresolved trauma she endured as a kid.

Bound to happen eventually, she believed as he was a fraternity brother to her sister sorority, who felt out-of-place because of his unorthodox rationale. He was smoking a cigarette after his fellow brothers teased him on his universal ideology of destiny and faith. They crossed paths during a night while she was puking in the sorority house's pool. He rushed over to make sure he held her hair back and didn't fall and drown in the pool.

The second time they crossed paths was the same night the potential alcohol poising discombobulated her. She almost endured when he rushed her to the hospital after fighting for her honor, when her sexual assault attacker tried to take advantage of her in the lounging area. In a typical perception of the Hollywood cliche, the sisters had joked with her saying, "These girls think they are Kardashian's, huh," as he used the napkin, he had in the back pocket of his fitted jeans to wipe the puke off her face.

"I look like shit, don't judge me, Papi," she said in a drunken slur.

Although the night only depicted flashes of the event, she remembered looking up at him in the back seat of the moving taxi and said, "Are you my Prince Charming to my Sleeping Beauty fairytale?"

She remembered hearing him say, "If you want me to be," and fading into black as he yelled in panic, "stay with me, Sleeping Beauty. Bro, speed it up. I can't afford to lose this one; she's special to me," and waking up in the hospital squinting to hear what the doctor was trying to say.

"Your wife suffered from severe alcohol poising and almost died on us. You reacted pretty well, son, in bringing her in immediately. They have already called the police to the sorority house and the fraternity house. They will be investigating. We get a lot of these incidents that happen there. I am glad you stepped up.

"Is she going to be okay?" she remembers him asking.

"She's going to be fine. We pumped her stomach and gave her charcoal, which will absorb the rest of the alcohol in her system. She will need some rest and some comforting, but she will be fine," the doctor reassured.

"Thank you, sir. Thank you for saving her. This girl means a lot to me."

Before blacking out again, she said to herself, "This dude has abandonment issues.

She remembered still being in a stupor hearing the conversation he had with her father that morning, which she wondered if he's even left the hospital yet. She heard her dad sobbing on the phone.

"She's okay, sir. She is recovering and will get released today. If it's okay with you and her, I am going to make sure she gets back to normal," he said empathetically.

"Thank you, Mijo, for taking care of my baby girl. I wish I were there to protect her," her father said in sobbing agony.

"That's why I am here, sir; she's precious cargo," he reassured him.

That day she remembered the lengths he went to ensure she recovered well. He made the most incredible chowder that always tasted like heaven with the bread that she swore came out of a Jiffy box with an extra kick. She remembered when she finally got off balance in her studio apartment; he rushed to her side to make sure she didn't fall.

"I realized you're a bit clumsy; I need to make sure you don't scare me as you did a few days ago," he said in a soft, deep, comforting voice.

She remembered the night terrors that followed the night after, which resulted in the next few days of her screaming, which started the continuation of the dream before going to work that night. The two back to back always gave her this sense of terrifying fear when they slept in the same bed. Every time the dreams occurred, he continuously reassured me with the strong, comforting arms of the six-foot-four-inch hunk of a man.

She remembered the feeling she had one night when she broke down in tears, and he immediately woke and held her half-naked body while saying in his sultry and deep comforting tone, "You're okay. You're okay. You're safe. I am always going to protect you, Sleeping Beauty.

For the first time in her life, she felt a sense of safety and protection. She felt like she was home, which was a feeling she lacked since her godfather and uncle passed away.

After the wounds healed, he continued to come around, which was odd for her. The two things that she adored about him was his consistency and that he was always a man of his word. He was noble and valiant, which was hard to encounter in this modern world. They became inseparable for the next few years, which, like any strong bond between two individuals who grow an admiration for one another, was love. She opened up, and with every argument she tried to start when she didn't get her way, he walked away. She fueled more and more on purpose, not because she wanted to hurt him intentionally, but because she knew she could. This made Carlos Herrera, before they knew him worldwide as Jonathan King, walk away from her life forever.

"How dare you say that I am worthless and an ungrateful man trying to control you," he said that one stormy week during the wake of Katrina. "How dare you say you wish that I were in New Orleans to give you peace? You want me gone, Princess; all you had to do was ask," he said, distraught, heartbroken, and in rage.

"No one's stopping you, Mr. King; it's no skin off my back," she said prudishly.

"Kiss my ass, princess," he said, heartbroken as he stormed out the door.

"Kiss my ass Charming," she yelled back in the pet name she gave him, expecting him to come back through the door, which was the reality when he didn't walk back in his usual fifteen seconds, making her tear up. She ended up rushing out the door in a frantic already thinking he was speeding off in the Balcones Heights Apartment she used to live in and found him in tears at the same spot he told her, "I love you, Princess.

When she saw him there remembering that day, her heart opened up, screaming in grief, "Charming, I'm sorry for being an evil bitch," which resulted in them running to each other meeting, with the iconic passionate kiss they always shared and cherished. Not the *Buffy the Vampire* lip lock, but *The Notebook* kind of kiss which was the first time they ever passionately united. Thinking about it took her breath taken away like it was the same day, and her legs shook while she felt the warmth bolting through her body.

He got recognized as the iconic Jonathan King, which the insecurities never settled in as everyone knew who Alessandra was. She earned praise for her sense of security in herself. She didn't worry after the job, and she got on the amateur set of the upcoming film company *Infliction.* Everyone respected her and Jonathan's love.

Having the ladies who became close friends with Alessandra tell her, "Girl, you inspire me to gain the love you and Jonathan have. You guys are a couple not to reckon with as you're a badass chick, and he's an amazing co-star who proves that people have nothing to fear when they have trust and love so strong.

Infliction gave him his big break, and he had to move to California.

The romance went strong for the next few years, which ended the night Carlos Rivera finally broke into the adult film industry. Her traumatic divorce wounds slowly eased away, which became a faint memory that she still fully didn't recover from; made apparent when he moved to Los Angeles, California. He didn't want to be without her, and neither did she. Still, the one thing stopping her was the life she had in San Antonio, which then she didn't understand what Jonathan meant when he said, "You have a family of grown adults. They can take care of themselves," which she took as him requesting to forget them.

"You know what, Johnny, you're not the man I thought you were. I can't marry you," she said apologetically.

"Oh, you're going to walk away from your destiny and turn your back on your happily ever after," he said, trying to hold his tears.

"I wish you the best, Charming. I know you're going to gain so much success," she said, also now holding back tears.

"Don't do this to me, Alessandra. I love you," he said, now breaking down in tears.

"I'll always love you, Charming. You're my person," she said, looking back as she walked away from the packed apartment, they once shared.

She could hear him break down in their empty Alamo Heights Apartment and held back the tears of grief that she fought so hard to hold back, which was short-lived as she walked out the apartment heading to her silver Toyota Prius. She cried ugly, wiping the black mess that was the eye makeup she wore from the going away party her friends had planned, being proposed to in front all her friends and close family, in the Tiffany blue box that she always wanted like in the movie *Sweet Home Alabama.* She sat in the car for five minutes, looking back at all the happy times she had during her life, dating a porn star. She cried even harder when the radio personality introduced the song that reminded her so much of the love story they shared - David Guetta and Usher's *Without You.* Her Android HTC pinged, and she saw the notification received from Charming with the beating heart emoji that read "Look at your window" and saw his heartbroken face and his "I love you gesture" he always gave to her. He opened her door and shared one last, *The Notebook* kiss, before she got the courage to say, "I'm going.

Driving off in the bright sun, looking in the rearview mirror, she watched him fall to his knees, looking back at her heartbroken. She shed a few silent tears as she remembered that day, realizing what happened had her come back to reality, which snapped her back at the moment with the ping alert from the Passeio mobile app that read, "Coming out now.

It was already 2:25 a. m. on the St. Mary's strip of San Antonio. After a busy rush that brought to her attention that the traffic died down, she had starred in with Jonathan King in her first debut as an *Infliction* guest was circulating in her "big city small town." The night was full of horny ass men and insulting women, which already had her blood boiling. After the long haul of derogatory and shameful treatment, she was thankful that this Passeio client was taking his sweet time.

She was wearing cut-off shorts she saw as a steal at Wal-Mart, which looked identical to the New Republic shorts that she used to wear in Houston, which resembled Daisy Dukes with her long stems and voluptuous rear. Shehad on a hot pink paisley high low chiffon tank top; she felt like a superhero every time she glided running errands on her breaks. She had her signature calf-high knock-off Converse shoes she purchased on Amazon on one of the Daily Deals for twelve bucks, smoking a cigarette in the arid morning breeze. She saw the door open, which immediately had her throw the cigarette butt down and step on the ignited half cigarette.

A puggy short man came walking to the car belligerent as fuck, already looking at her like she was a girl with daddy issues, and said in a cocky slurry tone, "Damn girl, I would like to get in between that fine ass.

"Excuse you," she said in an insulted tone. "Wait, don't tell me your Casanova," she said in an annoyed tone?

"Yeah, I am. I have a good tip waiting for you at the destination," he said, sure of himself.

"Look, Umpa Lumpa, I had a pretty fucked up night; let's keep it professional," she said rationally.

"Wait, you're Itza Hellfire," aren't you? Well, I think you could use a little love being brought down from Aztec royalty to a pitiful rideshare driver. Why don't you let big poppa make you feel good?" he confidently said as he reached for her ass.

Being avid in self-defense and tapping into her survival instinct, she deflected his plump hand, and with force, pinned him to the back passenger's side window. She grabbed him by the junk, which only required three fingers to secure, and pinned his fat body to the car, not realizing spectators were looking at the entire event play out.

"Look, Bobaphat, I had a rough and long shift. I'm PMS-ing, I haven't eaten, and my tolerance level is at I'm out of pendejadas for the day, don't try me. Considering the number of fingers I have securing the junk, I can single-handedly rip them out. I hate to break it to you, but your attempt to grab my ass makes this self-defense. There is nothing big going on down there," she said, holding her rage.

He cried in agonizing pain, which was dramatic as she applied no pressure or force to his pencil dick, and screamed, "Help me. This psycho slutty whore is trying to rape me.

A familiar voice responded and said firmly, "Careful who you're insulting, Bobaphat, that's my precious cargo there." The voice was sultry, deep, and all too familiar.

"Jonathan King, thank God you showed up. She went crazy on me. These sluts that drive for Passeio are always crazy," he cried, faking fear.

Alessandra let go immediately and whipped around as quickly as a guy pulling out and said, "Jonathan."The pudgy pants pencil dick tried to take a cheap jab by trying to slap her, which ended up having him pinned by a two hundred and fifteen pound muscled adult entertainer to the silver Rouge Nissan.

"I thought I told you, Bobaphat, you're insulting my person, my precious cargo. I hope you know you have a crowd watching the whole thing play out. I saw it play out. You almost grabbed my girl and the love of my life. Being charged as a sex offender and getting assault charges added to that is the least of your concerns. I am about to make you regret what you attempted to do to my girl and have a permanent reminder of why you shouldn't disrespect women again, especially my woman," he said firmly.

"I'm sorry, sir," which resulted in him running across the street and into an alley in panic, followed by a thud and shriek from what sounded like a damaging fall.

"Your girl, huh? Even after the last rendezvous in Houston.

"What did I tell you that day you drove off when you looked out your window? You're always going to be my person," he said in that loving voice he always had, even in Houston.

"I'm sorry I did that infamous vanishing act," she said gratefully, appreciatively, and unapologetic as she jumped up to hug his entire body.

"Hey, it's you. I'm used to it. It's your thing. It's what happens after we always cross paths," he said assuredly.

"Why do you always have impeccable timing, Charming," she said sarcastically and playful.

"I know when my princess needs her knight and shining armor," he said in that passionate, raspy, sultry voice.

They continued to embrace as they could never break apart when united like this. "Since I owe you a blowjob, does this mean that after we kiss, you're still not going to turn into a frog?" she asked, playfully unsure.

"Never. You know why?" he asked.

"Why?" she asked curiously.

"It's not just our love we have; it's destiny," he said as he embraced her in her favorite kiss of her lifetime, *The Notebook* kiss.

Chapter 5

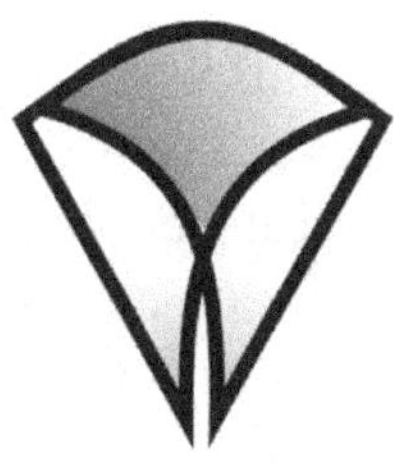

It about 2:30 a. m. when they arrived at their favorite cheap day spot, Lulu's Café, that July night. Jailhouse Café, the spot's former name, was the sister restaurant now known as the infamous Lulu's Café. Everyone knew them at this diner as the owner had been dealing with this star-crossed couple since their early college days after leaving their fraternity and sorority lives behind. This lifestyle was a simple institutional trap that the organization's highest-ranking controlled both felt. Since their plans to become married were never in the cards for their unofficial couple. In these organizations, destiny cannot be determined; they partook in their young, dumb, and full of cum days as freshmen in college. But since they are masters of their own destiny's, they felt in their hearts, they were a Romeo and Juliet, and their fates always kept them apart, until now.

"Good evening, Lucy," the couple said as they walked in and saw the owner working her crazy shifts as usual.

"OMG, what a pleasant surprise to see you both together, reunited once again. It must feel good to be back together," she said delightfully. "Are you guys again the unofficial couple you guys used to be, or are you lying to y'alls self, lying that you guys aren't?" she asked jokingly.

"You know how us crazy kids are," Alessandra recited back jokingly.

"It's great seeing you with that whimsical look you guys had back in college. You two belong together," she said in her usual playful and teasing tone. "How was Houston, Baby girl? Are you back for good or is this your usual visit?" she asked, hopefully.

"No, it's permanent this time. You know how it goes; shit hits the fan," she said in disappointment.

"Yeah, maybe she'll come to Los Angeles with me after my three-year project is over," Jonathan chimed in with that sweet, hopeful tone he had when he hinted at plans to marry her.

Alessandra looked at him, gleefully surprised.

In her usual psychobabble, Lucy said, "Well, you know kids, things happen for a reason.

"That's what I keep telling her, but you know Alessandra, she's more stubborn than a narcissist," he said jokingly.

"Hey, I'm still here, guys," Alessandra said playfully.

"Congratulations to the both of you on your rising stardom. My son is a huge fan of both of you," Lucy said proudly.

"Oh God, Lucy, don't remind me. The night was a bitch with that stupid video circulating during my Passeio shift this morning," she said in embarrassment.

"Nothing to be ashamed of, babycakes," Lucy reaffirmed. "You know Tommy; he's a film buff and an amazing critic," she reaffirmed. "He says your camera chemistry is very noticeable. And your love is undeniable for one another, even after so many years. You guys are the Romeo and the Juliet of the adult industry," she said confidently.

"Babe, I told you," Jonathan responded in excitement.

"Calling me Babe still, I see," Alessandra said condescendingly.

"Hey. Bad habits never die," Jonathan said proudly.

Lucy looked at them in admiration as she said, "You guys make a young widow want to go back and put herself on the market again." She touched Alessandra with that mother-like touch on her right shoulder, like she always did as she said, "It's a beautiful and normal act. It's more beautiful watching you too," she reaffirmed. "Let me get back to it and see if I can go home for once," she said jokingly. "Your usual spot," she asked conformingly.

"Yes, Lucy, the usual. Maybe I can convince her this one last time to fly away with me," Jonathan said whimsically like Ryan Gosling in *LaLa Land.*

"Yeah, maybe not," Alessandra said abruptly.

"Okay, you crazy kids. Let me prep your spot. And Alessandra," Lucy said.

"Yes, ma'am," Alessandra responded politely.

"Don't fight it, and don't get embarrassed. This man has been waiting to run into you since he moved back in May," she confirmed.

"Yes, ma'am. I'll try," she responded in her usual polite and adjugated tone.

She left to get her go-to cleaning agent, Lavender Fabuloso.

"So, when were you going to tell me you moved back? And when were you going to tell me you were here for the next three years," Alessandra asked in her usual defensive, you're hiding shit from me tone.

Jonathan shrugged and said, "When you asked me, I suppose.

Lucy escorted the two to their usual table - the middle, both near the window of the front of their cherished go-to spot and sat down.

Jonathan was in the adult industry but always presented himself elegantly with his signature fitted bootcut jeans, his button-down Express shirt in his now-signature color light blue, the color that the love of his life always complimented him, and now in a short almost military haircut. Jonathan was an old soul with symbolism frequently present, which was his way of telling the world and Alessandra, I still love you, girl. You're still my person.

"Are you getting your usual cheat meal, the Sherriff plate that you always share?" she asked in admiration.

"Why mess up a good thing," he said.

"What! You're controlling now?" Alessandra asked defensively.

"Where are my manners? What would you love, Princess?" Jonathan asked politely.

She thought for a minute and then had that adorable you're-right face he loved that made him smile cheek to cheek and said, "What he said. He's right.

Why mess up a good thing," she responded in disappointment.

Lucy sighed in admiration. "You got it.

They sat down at their usual spot, facing Lucy's on McCullough Street. Since they were Sagittarians, they both had their little setup routine, where Alessandra would set up the condiments she used according to order as her go-to habit was always eating the fries first and then the entrée after. Jonathan was the opposite of her. He set the utensils in the order of his attack.

"Here are your special plates, kiddos," Lucy said joyfully. "These plates have a special place in my diner for you," she proudly said as she pointed to the display on top of her most significant achievement, getting recognized by the Food Network.

Alessandra was wide-eyed and looked surprised as she said, "Wow ma, for us never to be united, there is hope for us.

"It's not high hopes, Alessandra; it's destiny. Your food will be right out, babycakes," she said as she winked at her and gave the plates and put them in front of them.

Alessandra looked at Jonathan and smiled.

Jonathan followed with, "Why are you so against destiny? You never told me why Princess Dodgy Pants."

"Why are you dodging the fact that you still yet haven't told me you were staying semi-permanently," Alessandra corrected sternly? "And why haven't you called me?" she added, a little hurt.

"I knew the video we did," he smiled coyly, "embarrassed you.

“Embarrassed, but not mad, Jonathan. You came through at my worst time. If it weren’t for that unexpected court case against the apartments in Houston, I would have been on the streets,” she added.

“No, Babe, you’ll never be on the streets. You would have only been on the streets because you wouldn’t have told Abuela,” he corrected with a smile.

“Okay, you know how I feel,” she corrected.

“Hey, you’re worth the sacrifice to Abuela, to all of us. You’re special,” he added.

“I’m not Jonathan; I’m just a girl who hasn’t gotten her shit together. I am a thirty-seven-year-old girl living with my Abuela,” she said in disappointment.

“You know you’re so cute when you’re beating yourself up like that,” he added in admiration.

Lucy came out of the diner's back with their signature ‘Sheriff Plate’ with a little extra surprise. The signature jumbo cinnamon roll that read in hot pink icing, “Welcome Home Romeo and Juliet.

“The cinnamon roll is on me; I hope you guys have room? And before you say anything, Alessandra, it’s on me,” she added gleefully.

“Thank you, Lucy. You’re giving us too much credit,” Alessandra said bashfully!

Jonathan looked at her with a cheery smile.

“Well, we know you’re kind of a penny pincher,” Lucy said.

Alessandra looked at her with that “really” face and followed with, “Yeah, you’re on point, Mami,” in a joking tone.

“How can you deny this boy? He brings the best out of you, babycakes. If you would just…”

Jonathan interrupted, "…Let's eat, shall we?"

Lucy looked at him and smiled. "Alright, dears, enjoy your meal and hope you like the cinnamon roll. I added a special ingredient for you too, lavender," she said happily. "It was the ingredient I added for the Valentine Day batch last year, and those couples are still going on strong. It's good luck," she added in a refreshing tone before she left to sit the only other two people in the diner.

They split the humongous plate in half, and before they split the plate, Alessandra inspected them.

"What is it, Babe" Jonathan asked.

"I think this is your plate," she said inquisitory.

"Flip it around," he added.

The initials of AR and JK inside a heart in red permanent marker were visible.

"I never noticed that," she said, surprised.

"You never do, Babe," he said as he dug into the sultry golden chicken-fried steak covered in the signature gravy. He began chewing in decadence as he said, "You are all about the little things in life, and you never noticed them," he said as he savored the crunchy goodness.

"Still a Gordo in disguise," she said.

"Hey, I love food," he said.

"Makes me wonder if you're even human after how much you eat and still look like a hot piece of ass," she added jokingly.

"Hey, I have feelings too, Babe," he said bashfully.

"And when did you get so rude, interrupting Lucy the way you did?" she said mother-like.

"Because you don't know when to shut up or stop being defensive," he said, correctively swallowing the first bite of chicken fried steak, which followed with a grin and continuous eyebrow raise.

"You're a jerk," she said with a pause. "But you're my jerk," she said with a grin. "Oh yeah, one more thing," she added.

"What is it, Babe," he said concerningly.

"Don't call me Babe," she added assertively.

He paused for a minute with a look that made Alessandra a little uneasy.

"Did I fuck up again?" she said cautiously.

He broke the grin with a smile and corrected her. "I can call you whatever I want," he said confidently. "Because you're my person," he added lovingly.

She looked at him for a second and smiled. She shut up and started chowing down.

Chapter 6

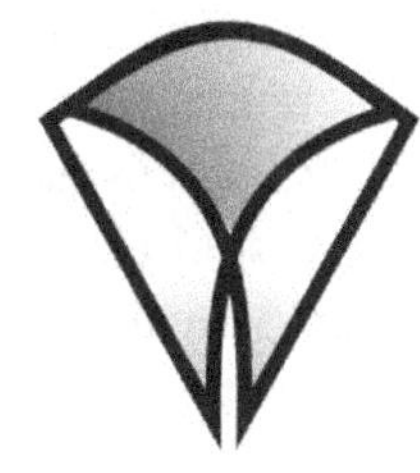

It was 6:00 a.m. the next morning when Alessandra woke up. She was not in her usual surroundings as she was in a room that almost looked like she was in the *Great Gatsby* film. She looked around frantically for a moment, checking to see if any articles of clothes were missing, if she had any bruises or wounds, and realized that she ended up coming to the new check-in hotel as Jonathan was already checking out of the suite he housed in initially.

It was charming and elegant all that at the same time. She noticed the rooftop composed of repurposed garbage articles with a vintage gray and gray hunter wallpaper with baroque print. The air smelled like lavender, which she resolved was the cinnamon roll. She looked at the side table on the side and found her keys, her phone, and a special surprise, the little blue Tiffany box. She heard the door open quickly and delicately close.

Jonathan could see the beads of sweat roll down the nape of her neck. He was wearing his San Antonio College hoodie that he swore he would never throw away as it was the beginning of his journey in meeting his person, he would tell her along with his basketball shorts that hugged his pelvis in every right way.

“Bad dreams again, Babe,” he asked empathetically.

“No, not at all,” she said sluggishly.

“At least the screams don’t happen anymore. It always broke me into pieces seeing the fear life has brought upon you,” he said as he walked to the bedside and took a seat with an overnight bag.

“Why didn’t you take the Rouge,” she asked, changing the subject.

“Because I didn’t have permission,” he said as he leaned in to give a kiss on the forehead.

“I don’t know why these dreams don’t stop,” she said with uncertainty.

“Are they the ones of the actual events or the ones with the beast you were afraid of?” he asked in concern.

“No, those dreams stopped after I faced that bullshit in Houston,” she confirmed apathetically.

“I was really worried about you for a while, Babe. It’s been one horrible tragedy after another, but what I admire about you the most is how you deal with it,” he assured.

“Come on, Jonathan, you always give me too much credit. I usually hold it in until I explode. That is why things always went bad between us. I wouldn’t feel. I would conceal,” she said mournfully. “Great, now I sound like fucken Elsa,” she said in disgust.

"Honestly, Babe, you deal with it in your own time. And that's okay. Because you deal with it, I give you enough credit as people hold it in forever. They end up enabling their inappropriate behaviors and make excuses for them. Keep to yourself, purposely walk on eggshells for a moment, and then deal with it to become a better person. That's what matters. Sure, you might push the love of your life away, but I don't take it personally. Yeah, I get hurt, but your emotional wellbeing matters the most. And bedside, I am not an entitled asshole, I understand. I mean, if you were like you say keeping up with the bills kind of girl, I would have walked away years ago," he reassured.

"Thanks, Babe," she said with a thankful tone.

"Wow, you called me Babe already; I am flattered," he said as he reached in for an actual kiss. "Call Abuela; she was a little concerned about you, which is why she's been blowing up your phone," he said concerningly.

"Why," she asked, concerned. "Before you answer that, why is this box on my nightstand? I thought you would have gotten rid of it by now since it didn't appear in Houston," she asked inquisitively?

"To be respectful of your order, well, it's yours. I bought it for you. Houston wasn't a time to return it to its rightful owner, and that was your moment, not mine. You would have taken it as another proposal, which wouldn't have been. It feels right; you have it. To answer the original question, they found two Passeio drivers brutally murdered, so she naturally thought it might have been you since we forgot to call her to let her know you were safe. I was selfish. We should have dropped by before we came to the hotel," he said in shame.

"Jonathan, you're always so hard on yourself. Don't you think you're also hard on yourself? It's time to take your advice, don't you think?"

"I lost my parents a long time ago. Your family means the world to me," he replied.

"Was she okay? Did she look upset," she asked in agony?

"She saw the car pull up, thinking it was an investigator to deliver bad news. I saw her looking out the window. When she saw me get out, she ran to the car in tears and thanked me for keeping you safe. You know, Abuela, she smacked me on the shoulder and told me we should have at least called," he assured.

"Was my dad and Tia okay? Did they look concerned," she asked?

"Of course, you're our girl. As soon as I walked in, your Tia prayed in tears, saying thank you for keeping you safe. And your dad greeted me with a big hug in mourning, thanking me for keeping his little girl safe," he reassured.

"Ever since college, he always saw you as the son he never had. Shit, he was mad at me for a week and told me how dare I hurt his future son," she reaffirmed, in the mocking tone her dad expressed that day. "Let me call them and apologize," she replied.

"Great idea. I brought the dress that I love seeing you in, by the way," he added.

Before making the call, she quickly skimmed through the text messages and saw the message from Passeio that read, "Important Safety Message." She promptly picked up the phone and dialed her contact labeled "La Familia Romero."

It rang once when Abuela picked up the phone, saying in anger, “Pinche cabrona, why didn’t you call and tell us you were with Carlos Culera?” which ended in mournful tears.

“Abuela, I’m so sorry,” Alessandra said, tearing up.

“Do you know the grief this family went through wondering if you were one of those girls killed?” she added in mournful tears.

Alessandra cried.

“I’m sorry, Abuela, you know shit like this doesn’t happen in San Antonio often,” she replied in mourning.

“This is not the same world anymore, Mija, you know that,” she replied.

“I guess I didn’t think of that possibility, as we always assumed Houston was worse than San Antonio,” she replied.

“Alessandra,” her dad replied, picking up the phone with hope.

“Daddy, it’s me,” she responded, crying harder now.

“Are you okay? Are you hurt? Did anything happen before you ran into Carlos,” he asked in concern.

“Other than the confrontation that Jona… I mean Carlos, the night was okay,” she replied as she sniffled.

Her dad cried while saying, “I thought we would never see you again.”

“I’m sorry, Daddy, I’m so sorry,” she replied.

“Thank God you’re safe,” he added.

Abuela sucked up the llargimas as she returned to normal serious safe and replied, “So you’re going to stay with Carlos tonight and bunker up because I know you’re not working tonight.”

Alessandra also sucked up the tears and went into challenge mode with her Abuela. "Why wouldn't I Abuela, I have bills to pay, I have a phone to pay for, I have to get my life back on track."

Jonathan added in the background, "…I already took care of your T-Mobile bill," he reassured.

"Did Abuela make you?" she asked, distraught.

"No, Mija. I didn't; he offered since we all agree it's dangerous right now," her father assured, sniffling from the grief.

"But what about my other bills, Daddy? We surely can't depend on Jonathan to save your irresponsible and stupid little girl, now can we?" she said in disappointment.

"You selfish little…" Abuela was about to say in anger until Jonathan chimed in the background.

"…Look, we know how you are, so I will ride with you tonight. I have that thing with the production company. We'll go back to it in between. You might not be armed, according to Passeio, but I can. I'm your bodyguard for the night," he assured everyone.

"We have a plan, Abuela. Look, I'm sorry for being disrespectful. You know I don't say the right things in my emotional outbursts. Look, I know you're afraid, and I get it. But you underestimate how much of a badass I can be. I mean, look at me now, I took on and conquered the big city, and I was alone. The crime rate was much higher. You don't think I chauffeured a serial killer or two. It's all about boundaries and letting people know that I'm a person not to even try it with," she reassured everyone listening.

Jonathan gave that concerned and agreed nod he always gave when he was sure but still skeptical.

"You're right, Princessa. You're the only thing we got. We would die if anything happened to you. I am sorry for insulting you," Abuela replied.

She heard the other line hang up, which was the sign that Abuela took control of the situation.

"Look, Abuela, I'm going to be okay. Uncle Mike trained me pretty well on the self-defense side. I've handled the big city and survived. And as extra comfort, Carlos will ride with me. Have faith, and don't worry," she reassured.

"You're right, Mija. And thank you for apologizing; be careful out there, okay. And Carlos, we are not stupid in not knowing about the little video you guys did. She's a target. You protect her, or else you will have to worry about this crazy bitch," she confirmed.

"Don't worry, Abuela, she'll be safe. I promise," he assured.

"Alright, Abuela, let me at least start earlier than I do. Let me let you go so I can hit the road and be off no later than midnight. I love you," she assured.

"I love you too, Mija," she replied in an unsure fear.

Alessandra hung up the phone, put it on the nightstand, opened the box, and put it on her left index finger.

"You're going to wear it," he said joyfully.

She picked up her overnight bag he collected and started walking to the shower. She turned and gave him an air smooch and said, "Yes. It's for good luck and protection." She closed the door behind her.

Jonathan heard the shower turning on and looked up to the roof and recited, "Please protect her tonight. Please make sure she's special. reassure me she's ready."

Chapter 7

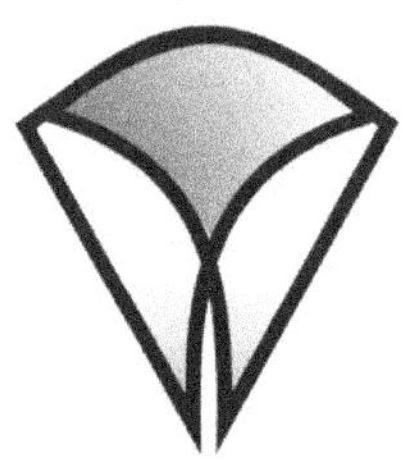

It was about 8:15 p.m. when they arrived at the Revolution Production Studio. Jonathan was filming a commercial for the new upcoming talent search for *Mi Gente*, a Latin spinoff that was a hybrid of *The Voice* and *American Idol*. A celebrity personality would aid the final round of competitions in the music industry that would crown the *Mi Gente* competition's final winner. As soon as they arrived at the Production Studios, the phone pinged with the iconic, whimsical beep from Passeio.

"Dammit, I forgot to get offline," she said, disappointed.

"Reject it," Jonathan said quickly.

Alessandra picked up the phone to see the request, which had in bold at the top "Guaranteed hundred-dollar ride excluding tip," and her eyes opened in shock.

"I never got one of these rides," she said in amazement.

"It sounds kind of sketchy," Jonathan replied.

She accepted to see where she had to pick up the ride. Since she was a Ruby driver, it also advanced the general area, the same area as the production studio.

She flipped the phone to show Jonathan and replied, "Look, it's a pickup at the Marriot Downtown, which comes in the same area, with one stop at that video store with the dark tin on Broadway," she affirmed. "I am sure it's one of your fans who found out you're filming today and wants you to sign a DVD," she reassured.

He looked at the duration time of the trip. "Only a fifteen-minute duration," he said. He gave that unsure look and that same uneasy nob. "Okay, Alessandra, activate your Family Locator feature. If you're not back in fifteen, I'm out of here quicker than the Flash," he said firmly.

"Okay, Babe," she said flirtingly.

"Wow, you called me, Babe! Winning," he replied as he reached for a kiss before getting out of the car. He kissed her long and kissed her hard; she stopped to look at him.

"Jonathan, nothing is going to happen, don't get paranoid."

"I don't know what I would do if anything happened to you," he said in concern.

"You're going to be late. Hurry, you have a commercial to film," she said.

He reached in for one last kiss and got out of the car with that worried look he had. She remembered flashes during their college years when she didn't almost make it.

He was wearing a button-down dress shirt with a royal blue tie, tuxedo pants, and a black sports coat.

"Hey, Charming," Alessandra screamed out the car.

Still looking at her vehicle to see her drive off, he said, "Yes, Princess.

"Has anyone told you you look like Pitbull in that snazzy outfit?" she said jokingly.

"Ha, ha, hilarious. I hate that guy," he said in resentment.

"Why?" she asked in a confused tone.

"Because he's the only guy that might steal my person away since you are so in love with that guy," he said in disappointment.

She smiled and shrugged her head and said, "You're so silly," in an amused tone. "No one's taking me away from my Prince Charming," she reassured.

He smiled and waved as she started turning the corner of the street the studio was located. She slowed down to give him another air kiss that he returned and then yelled, "I Love You.

She replied, "I love you more, and yes, I'll marry you," she said as she sped off.

Jonathan immediately jumped for joy, looking up at the sky screaming, "Fuck yes. Thank you, universe, for finally giving in to our destined love story. Universe, I owe you one," he shouted in delight.

***

Allessandra arrived at the Marriot Downtown near River Center Mall around 9:45 p. m. She was wearing a hot pink chiffon dress with rose gold marbled markings that she designed and made during her college years at the

University of Incarnate Word that fit as she swore she was getting fat. The Passeio app pinged with a message that read, "be down in 5 minutes," which was the perfect time for Alessandra to get off, take off her four-inch stilettos, which she got at a steal from Ross Dress for Less on Commerce, and lit up the cigarette. She thought about the decision she made and smiled, which led her to think of all the possibilities. The message ping from the Passeio app that said, "Coming down," halted her thoughts. All smiles, she took one last drag of the half-smoked cigarette and went on the passenger side to open the back passenger door. She looked down to locate the handle, and as she looked up, she immediately went into shock. In her dream, the guy she had turned into the beast wearing the same thing in her dream approached the open door, sat in the seat, and took it upon himself to close the door.

Alessandra smiled politely, walked toward the car's backside, and said to herself, "Holy shit," in fright. She played it off that she fell and while for a split second whispered to herself, "Get it together, bitch.

She entered the vehicle and marked the passenger as en route.

"Everything okay?" he said in a deep and cold tone.

"Yeah, clumsy. Clumsier now since I just said yes to my boyfriend," she said while flashing a grin.

The passenger flashed an icy grin and said, "Good."

"So, we're heading to your first stop. Where is your ultimate destination?" she asked, keeping calm.

"Destiny," he replied as he looked the other way.

The phone rang the assigned ringtone, *Moon River*, which was Jonathan's set ringtone.

She picked up the phone. "Is everything okay?"

"Yeah, Charming. Heading to the first stop and then headed to the final destination," she answered, trying to conceal her fear.

"Okay, Princess. I am almost done at work. I'll be ready by the time you finish," he said ignorantly.

"Okay, we reached the first destination already, so I should there soon," she said uneasily.

"Okay, I will see you soon. Love you," he replied.

"Love you too," she answered before hanging up the phone.

The passenger turned toward her mechanically in slow motion, like one of those mechanical dummies you see at Chucky Cheese when they are ready to malfunction, and replied, "How cute" in the same deep monotone and impersonal voice and got out of the car.

Alessandra waited for him to enter the video store and, when he wasn't in sight, immediately activated the safety feature on the app, which marked "911 follow the ride."

He immediately came out of the video store holding one giant sack and one smaller plastic black bag.

"Found what you were looking for?" Alessandra asked politely.

"More than I bargained for," the passenger replied in the same tone.

The tone gave Alessandra goosebumps and a shiver, which was the same feeling she had before being sexually assaulted in Houston. There is something about that feeling you get when something seems eerily wrong, which Alessandra said was the natural Spidey sense we all get when we feel trouble is about to happen that we naturally talk ourselves out of. Since after the college incident, she took notice of the feeling. Since Houston, she never avoided it as it was her safety net.

"Take a turn through Brackenridge Park," the passenger responded.

With the safety feature and Find A Family Member activated, she replied, "No problem." She had her eyes on the passenger through the rearview mirror, making sure she focused on his every move. Her palms became sweaty, and her pulse pounded harder and harder while thinking to herself, *I'm going to die tonight*. She glanced at the road. It was only seconds after that she heard a honk and then tasted iron in her mouth. She looked at her mirror and saw the passenger attempt to swing again, which immediately had her swerve the opposite way, throwing back the passenger as he thudded and shattered the glass. She quickly reached for her stiletto; the passenger attempted to lunge at her with a knife; she impaled the stiletto into his eye until she heard a pop.

The passenger yelled for a split second, saying, "You bitch" and attempted to lunge at her and stabbed her in the shoulder.

"You pussy ass motherfucker," she yelled as she accelerated to full speed. The road bent, and she crashed into a tree. She felt the airbag hit her face, causing the iron taste in her mouth to return, and blacked out for a split second. The car was now the size of a two-door hatchback. She opened her smashed door, using her weight to open the door. She stumbled out of the vehicle, feeling weaker by the second as she attempted to run for her life. She was losing too much blood. She felt woozy, followed by a sharp pain in her back. felt the warmth of blood protruding out of the wound; she screamed in agony. She had enough strength to lift herself and do a back kick that followed with a painful groin. She was losing too much blood to get up completely. She crawled to reach for help and felt her body flip over, looking at the one-eyed passenger.

"Who are you," she asked, feeling the life escaping your body.

"Your worst nightmare, you fucken cunt," he said in anger.

All she remembered was feeling the pain of the cold blade entering her body and a glow before she blacked out. When she opened her eyes, she saw Jonathan's face and feeling gushes of wind hitting her body. "You always have impeccable timing," and blacked out.

She saw her Uncle Mikes' figure approaching her saying, "It's your time warrior," and blacked out again. When she finally woke up, she ejected up, screaming and looking at her surroundings. She found herself on the side of a lagoon that looked like the cavern she visited in New Braunfels during her elementary school field trip at Loma Park Elementary but in the pool with a lagoon with a blue glow. She examined her body as she felt sore but couldn't distinguish if this was reality or fantasy. She immediately panicked and screamed, "Jonathan Carlos," and heard the echo of his voice in the background. She saw Jonathan naked, and to her dismay, drenched in blue flames. As he approached her, she felt the flames' heat, but they weren't burning her.

"Your safe, Babe, your safe," he said, reassuring. "How do you like me in these flames? Pretty cool, huh?" he said confidently and revealed his true identity.

"I'm dreaming, right?" she asked, freaking out.

He smiled his usual smile and replied, mimicking *The Weeknd* saying, “I’m a mother fucken Star Boy,” and revealed one of his supernatural powers, transporting them from the cavern to an infinite room, revealing the Universe right in front of her eyes.

She looked at him with a severe and stern face and replied, “No way,” before she fainted.

Chapter 8

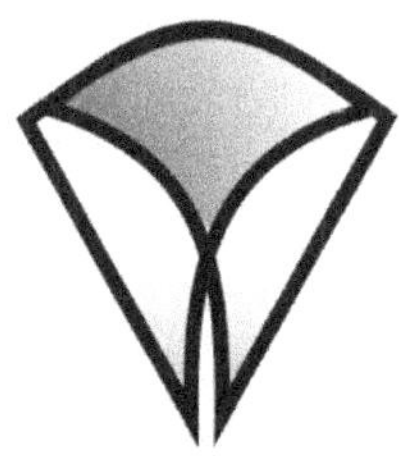

She opened her eyes and found herself face-to-face with the beast again, as it cocked its neck back yet again.

"I didn't teach that one, Mija," Uncle Mike said excitedly this time.

"Lara Croft never failed me then; she will not fail me again," she said this time a lot more confidently but extremely confused.

"You didn't act cocky this time. Great progress," he said proudly. "What now?" He asked inquisitively.

She crouched low as she saw the Beast erect two heads and screamed, "Element of mother fucken surprised," she said as she waited to see the beast's next move.

The Beast looked adjacent as he saw what Alessandra's next move. The creature looked at his twin's head and hissed. They looked down, waiting to see Alessandra's next move.

Alessandra smiled at the Beast and waved, saying, "Hey sexy, what's popping" as she skipped to the other side.

"Alessandra, this is no time for fun and games, girl," Uncle Mike scolded.

"Just wait and see Uncle Mike," she reassured.

The beast belted a loud and now aggressive roar that shook the boulder, making some boulders fall to the ground. In anger, the beast cocked his now two heads up and speared for her.

"Here goes nothing." She kissed her fingers, pointing to the sky, and waited to roll back. What was a ground roll turned into a backflip jump. She turned to look at the beast rammed into each other's head from a six-foot radius.

"FUCK YEAH," Uncle Mike roared!

"Holy fuck, I just pulled a Lara Croft," she said in shock.

"Is that what we call a superhero move?" Uncle Mike said proudly.

"Holy fuck!" She landed perfectly, supporting her landing by the hand distribution of her left hand. "When did I become Shera?" she said in amazement.

"You want to be Shera; you got it," Uncle Mike said jokingly.

What happened next blew her mind as she saw a sword and shield falling from the sky, landing perfectly into the ground between a distorted beast and her new weapon request.

"Holy fuck, I'm a mother fucken badass now," she said in wow. She crouched to wait for the beast to gain its consciousness and waited for the next attack.

The beast was livid, both heads eyeing her, and attempted to trap her in a compromising death.

"Now focus, Princessa, the next jump engages the Science geek and Physics geek I used to tease you about," Uncle Mike said in hope.

She made that WTF face and said, "Really?"

"Focus, girl," he scolded.

She tuned immediately into gravity and the Law of Physics, reciting Newton in her head, keeping both eyes on the Beast. She noticed one particular characteristic that she recalled from the last instance. Anytime the beast was about to attack, its second spiked scale vibrated. As soon as she saw that and saw his neck cock back again, this time aggressively, she jumped, intending to do a ground roll. She looked down and realized that thinking about the Law of Physics, she had more control of her maneuvering and landing. She recited the Law of Gravity, remembering the equations she despised so much and saw what happened next. The Beast impaled its second head right between the eyes.

"Fuck yes, Tio, I am a fucken Superhero," she said excitedly. "Now what goes up must come down," she said as she gracefully landed in front of the armory and pulled it out of the plateau of the boulder.

"Damn baby girl, this role suits you well," Uncle Mike said proudly.

Before she grabbed her shield, she put the sword between her legs and pulled off the ring.

"This is no time to do a costume change, Mija," Uncle Mike said confusingly.

"It's not a costume change; it's for protection," and put it on her left ring finger, grabbed the shield, and examined it quickly.

"YES," Uncle Mike roared in cheer.

She saw the beast in a quick morn of the doom of the twin head and roared in anger.

"Remember that saying that I would say when you were in pain," Uncle Mike quizzed.

"Sana?" Alessandra asked, confused.

"No, not that one," Uncle Mike scolded in embarrassment.

The Beast cocked its head back and inhaled as she saw an orange glow turn into a larger flame by the second.

"This doesn't look good, Uncle Mike," she said in fear.

"Say it now," he yelled in command.

"Si Se Puede con Los raizes de mi Gente" she yelled in unsure confidence as she put the shield in front of her to deflcct the flame. It fascinated her as the shield glowed, absorbing the flames that she could see from the hybrid hieroglyphics that appeared Aztec, Mayan, and Grecian.

"That's my girl," he cheered.

"What is it doing, and what are these symbols?" she asked as she fought the force of the remaining flame.

"You'll see, and it will all be revealed in good time," he reassured.

As soon as he finished, the last blast of flames turned into a deflection of the flame that ended, hitting the beast right in the kisser. screeched in agonizing pain as it caught flames.

"THAT'S MY GIRL," Uncle Mike continued to cheer.

"Damn, if I knew this was a weenie roast, I would have worn something more appropriate," she mocked as she saw the beast fall limp.

"So, the question I am dying to know, are you marrying the boy, finally?" Uncle Mike asked inquisitively.

"Carlos?" Alessandra asked.

"Yes, of course."

"We know I have issues, and they weren't daddy issues, that's for sure," she said reassuringly, and at that moment, she felt the boulder shaking. "What's going on, Uncle Mike?" she said in concern.

"Oh no, it's trouble. Quickly get off the boulder," he said in alarm.

She quickly jumped. She accelerated. She closed her eyes, thought about the equation in her head, found the solution, and saw other equations in her head. She felt the acceleration weaken, which made her open her eyes to see the park's entire ground shaking. She felt an uneasy feeling as she whispered to herself in fear, "THE APOCALYPSE."

"Yes, Mija, it's here," Uncle Mike said in fear.

As she landed gracefully, she looked around, seeing that the fog was gathering together, revealing the night's glowing sky. The ground shook even more violently. The ground was cracking open right before her eyes as the fog condensed into a dark and smoke like figure revealing the Aztecs' markings. As she squinted to gain focus, she saw the jewels that resembled the Aztec God's markings of Death. She felt a hand holding her legs out as they climbed out of the ground. They were holding her down while the rest of its body came out of the ground. She recognized the grim and familiar faces; it was the camping couple she passed in the first occurrence, which now took her to what was now the ledge of the divided ground.

"Uncle Mike, a little help here," she cried with no reply.

They held her in place while the figure approached her on the other side of the ledge.

"I've been waiting for this for a lifetime," the figure responded.

"Did you raid your cheap slutty mom's closet, or do you just have poor taste?" she said, concealing her fear in rage.

The outline of the same creepy grim smile appeared on what appeared to be the face of the dark man. "Your soul shall be mine," it said in a fierce and haunting way.

She felt her body fall into the crater, and as she dropped deeper, she saw an orange-red glow and panicked.

"Ugh, hello, Law of Physics," she heard Jonathan's smart-ass tone in the background.

"Jonathan?" she said in confusion.

His face appeared a few inches away from her view, and she saw his angelic and coy smile that would always pop up during her stab at Physics that she took for fun. "Hey, Warrior Princess," he said proudly.

She closed her eyes as she felt the heat of the molten rock as heard the gurgles of the boiling magma.

Chapter 9

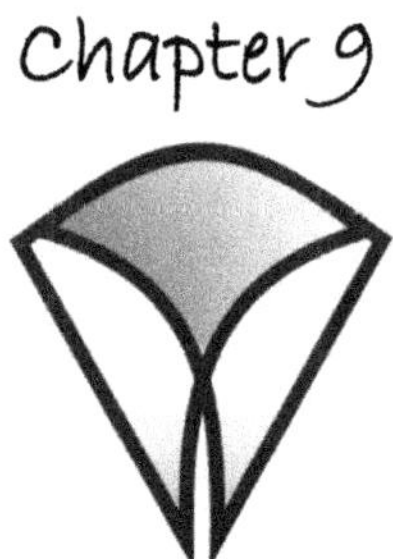

Alessandra ejected up again, gasping and touching her body to see if she was a hot melted mess. She looked around. She heard the familiar sound of Jonathan coming into the room with her favorite drink from Starbucks, her usual Venti Matcha Tea, and a thank you plastic bag that had a familiar smell, the Sheriff Platter from Lulu's.

"Good evening, Princess," he said joyfully.

"Oh, thank God, it was a dream," she sighed in relief.

Her phone rang, and as she reached for it, she noticed the diamond ring on her left hand's ring finger.

"Congratulations," her Abuela said in joyful praise.

"Ugh, thanks, Abuela, you all okay," she asked, confused.

"Put the phone on speaker," she said as she heard the other phone pick up, which was her dad.

Her dad busted with an immediate, "Welcome to the family, son!"

"Thanks, Mr. Romero," Jonathan said politely.

"Call me, Dad, son. You're part of the family now," her father said in joyful bliss.

"Thanks, Mr. Rome… uh Dad," while Jonathan signaled Alessandra to say something.

"Thanks, Daddy," Alessandra said politely, confused.

So, did you plan the date yet?" Abuela asked eagerly.

"No, the night was a blur. I just woke up," she said, dumbfounded.

"Well, I am sure you all pa…" her father was about to say until Abuela interrupted.

"…Shut up, Joseph," she said scoldingly.

"Well, Mija, you and Carlos have a lot to talk about, so we will get out of out your hair so you can talk," Abuela insisted.

"Alright, Abuela, I love you all," she said hesitantly.

"Okay, Mija, we'll talk soon; there is so much to talk about. I love you too," she reassured.

She hung up the phone and immediately said what was on her mind. "Jonathan, the dream continued this time," she said, worrisome.

"What happened, Princess Love?" he now called her since they were officially engaged.

"Well, remember the campers I told you about that ended up screaming when I was on top of the boulder on trail three," she said in dismay.

"Yeah," he confirmed.

"Well, they were zombies, or some fucked up version of *The Walking Dead.* And there was this fog-like figure with a knockoff of a reject version of the beautiful crown that she won on Miss Gay San Antonio," she said, mourning her lost friend.

"Yeah, the awesome chick that always gave me a peck on the cheek and said I better take care of her girl," he added.

"Yeah, well, he had his goons throw me into the divided ground after a crazy ass earthquake. And I had a sword made of jade and a shield that glowed when I deflected the flames; the two-headed turned one after I tricked it and had it kill his circle jerk buddy that glowed Aztec, Mayan, Grecian symbols that ended up firing back the flame," she said in confusion.

"Wow, you killed the beast on this one as he walked to the window to shade the room with the blackout curtains and continued to sit on the side of the bed where she was still laying in the tattered hot pink dress, she wore.

"And the passenger I picked up ended up in my dream too. But the first one," she said frantically.

"What do you mean?" he asked, eager to hear the rest of the story.

"The guy in my first series of dreams, he was my passenger!" she said, panicked.

"And he stabbed me in the shoulder rather than in my back. It felt like it went through my chest." She slowly looked down.

"I'm listening," he said, interested.

"Wait, why is my strapless off and a hole in my dress covered in what looks like blood?" she asked. "Was I that fucked up?" she asked, alarmed.

"We didn't go out, Princess. I had to help you," he said coyly.

"Help me with what?"

"Go on with the story. We might make it a movie with my connections," he said without hesitation.

"Okay," she said until she remembered Jonathan's part in the dream. "Oh. and remember that fucked up night in college?" she added without hesitation.

"Babe, I thought I was going to lose you that night," he added, resenting the night.

"Okay, well, the flashes came back but different flashes," she said in a hurry.

"What happened in the flashes?" he asked, extremely tuned in to the conversation.

"Well, I felt a consistent gush of wind. Then I woke up in a cavern, like the one you take me to when I need to remember my more innocent times. There were a glowing blue lagoon and a waterfall. I panicked because I thought some evil shit abducted me and yelled your name. And you responded, and you were in blue flames. And you showed me the Universe and said jokingly, I'm a mother fucken Star Boy," she said in fright.

"Warrior Princess," he said proudly.

"Wait, you called me that in the dream," she said, freaking out of her mind.

"Did I at least give The Weeknd justice saying that?" he asked intuitively.

Alessandra pulled back a little and replied, "I think he would have been proud. Why are you asking?" she said with caution and hesitation.

Jonathan got up to reassure her she was safe, like the last time she ended having a random episode when he accidentally triggered the trauma, she endured during college.

"Babe, let me reassure you. You're safe. You're in excellent hands," he said.

She tried to move back further but couldn't. "Jonathan, what are you not telling me?" she asked, now petrified.

A familiar voice chimed in her mind and said, "Mija, he's one of the good guys."

She said out loud in confusion, "Uncle Mike?"

"Yes, Mija," he reassured.

"Oh, my fucken God, it wasn't a dream," she said out loud.

"Yes, it was, but technically training," Jonathan reassured.

Alessandra freaked out. "What is happening?"

"Jonathan Carlos, can you show her she's not dreaming," Uncle Mike said affirmatively.

"Yes, sir, I'm on it. Let me take this shirt off. Your goddaughter gave it to me on our unofficial second anniversary," he said concerningly.

"Jonathan, Charming, you hear him too. Please tell me this is all a dream," she said in fear.

Jonathan got up shirtless, exposing his perfectly sculptured pecs and his washboard abs. He spread his arms out, revealing his perfectly sculpted biceps as he glowed a light blue glow that immediately busted into blue flames, slowly revealing his endowed sculpted body.

"Oh, my God. You are a mother fucken Star Boy," as Alessandra bumped her head on the carved golden headboard in the fancy hotel at the Pearl Brewery, but with a slight difference. Her body was out, but her senses were conscious.

Jonathan walked over to the bed, dis-ignited his blue flaming body, and sat on the bed as he lifted her head and kissed her.

"My sleeping Warrior Princess, wake up," he said jokingly.

She could still hear him.

Uncle Michael signed and replied annoyingly, "Mijo, she fainted."

She felt her body being adjusted as he placed her head on the pillow.

"Guys, you're going to talk shit after I can still hear you guys," she said telepathically.

"Babe, you gained your new power, yaaaayyy," Jonathan said in a whispered surprise.

"Mijo, you're not helping," Uncle Mike chimed in embarrassment.

"Oh, my bad, sorry, Babe," he said in the same joking whisper.

"Babe," Jonathan replied in confusion. "Warrior Princess," he repeated in uncertain confusion.

"Mijo, she's completed fainted," Uncle Mike sighed.

She gained her new power, yaaaayyy," he said in an embarrassed, jokingly tone.

Chapter 10

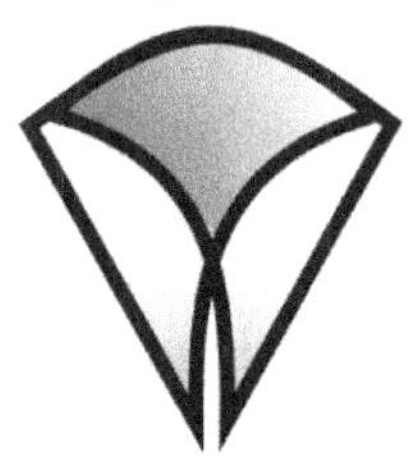

It was about 10:45 a.m. the following morning when Alessandra woke up from her fainting episode. She recalled feeling the thud when she hit the mounted headboard from what she continued to believe was a dream. She looked behind her to see the damage she might have caused. As she looked back, she saw the cavern wall in the ten-foot space she laid, a moss six-foot platform, and began to exam her base. She had a pillow on the section she was laying her head on surveying her surroundings.

She thought to herself in disappointment, *Great the fucken cavern again.* She got up from the one-foot platform to check her body for any unconventional bumps and bruises. "At least I am not missing a limb or anything."

She walked toward the lagoon with the rushing waterfall that glowed and glistened like a sapphire in the night.

"This is breathtakingly beautiful," she said. *It's incredible*. "Where am I?"

"We are in the underneath cavern at the Japanese Tea Garden," Jonathan's voice echoed in the background.

"Jonathan?" she asked in confusion. "Where are you," she asked in suspicion.

"I am in the training and armory section we made for you," Jonathan responded with caution.

"Why are you hiding like a predatory stalker then?"

"Because you reached your next level of powers, Mija," Uncle Mike's voice echoed in the cavern.

"Uncle Mike, am I hearing you, or are you in my head again?" she asked in confused delight.

"You hear my hearing voice, Princessa," he said, assuringly.

"Are you physically here?" she asked in hopeful confusion.

"With the help of Jonathan, of course," he said empathetically.

"Babe," Jonathan said happily as he came from the corridor of the cavern that followed with a golden force as Alessandra turned.

She looked at the golden light following her movement that ricocheted Jonathan to the caddy corner wall of the cavern, having him imprint his body on the wall with force.

"Holy fuck!" Alessandra said as she was inspecting her body to investigate where she secreted the forceful golden force. She examined herself until she heard the painful groans from Jonathan.

"Babe," she said as she ran to help Jonathan up.

"High Warrior Babe," he said in a groan as he pushed Alessandra from the pain she was causing him on the shoulder he landed on.

"I'm sorry, Babe. Did I fuck you up again," she asked concerningly?

He smiled at her in pain and said, "Yay, you got your other powers," as he groaned further.

"Why am I getting a nephew-in-law who's such a pussy?" a voice echoed that sounded familiar.

Alessandra recognized the too familiar voice. She looked back, and for a moment, she was in shock and then whimpered, which slowly turned into joyful tears. "Uncle Mike," she said as she wept harder.

"Alessandra, it's me," Uncle Mike replied, now six feet away from her.

Her body went limp as she cried even harder. "Is it you?" she asked in mournful uncertainty.

He walked up to her and gently put his hands on each shoulder as he whimpered, "I missed you so much, Mija."

She threw her hands around the six-two figure man as they both took a moment and sobbed.

Jonathan lifted himself and dusted off his body from the rock dust and said, "Yaaaayy family reunion. Can I bring out the champagne now?"

They both looked at him and looked at each other as they broke away from their embrace, wiping the tears out of their eyes.

Uncle Mike looked at Alessandra thoughtfully, asking, "Are you sure you want to marry this guy?"

Alessandra looked up at her Uncle, smiled, and looked at Jonathan for about thirty seconds, seeing Jonathan's joyful face slowly turn into an oh shit face.

"Babe, are we still engaged or not?" he said, concerned.

She looked at him seriously and asked, "What are you?"

"I told you, Babe, a Star Boy, well technically I am an Astron," and the sssshhhhh from Alessandra quickly interrupted him.

She looked at her Uncle Mike and chided, "I am marrying a mother fucken Star Boy deal," as she walked to Jonathan to embrace him with a hug, which he met with a happy grin and a five-second *Notebook* kiss. She pivoted to her uncle and said firmly, "If you don't like it, Bye Felipe."

He gave that playful look full of rage that he gave to her as a little girl that he could never keep straight, still trying to be mad at the situation, saying, "You know his kind is…"

"…Hey, sir." Jonathan starred at Uncle Mike. "I'm a badass, but I still have feelings here. Hey, after putting up with your bullshit, I…"

"…Hey, he's my Uncle and my second dad. Can you have respect and not wake me up from my dream here," which followed a slight pinch on the shoulder that followed with a painful "ouch," from Alessandra. "Holy shit, I am not dreaming," she said in shock.

"You will not faint again, are you Mija?" Uncle Mike said jokingly.

She wept and ran back to Uncle Mike's arms. "You're here.

“Yes, my sweet child, I am here for real,” he reassured in comfort.

It was hard for Alessandra to let go as she continued to weep even more.

“Hey son, can you come to get your girl before I cry again as well,” he said, already whimpering.

“Sorry, sir, she had me at it's you,” as he whimpered a little.

She looked back at Jonathan in tears as she reached for Jonathan who followed the gesture and came in for a hug.

Uncle Mike wept as he wrapped his left hand over Jonathan, saying, “Thank you for keeping her safe, son.

“Of course, she’s my person, sir,” he said in whimpers.

“Both of my protectors are here. Thank you, Lord, for this amazing blessing. ”She looked up at the glistening crystallite sprinkled in the cavern roof.

Uncle Mike, still whimpering, said, “Welcome to the family motherfucker.”

“Mother fucken Star Boy,” Alessandra admonished, correcting him.

Chapter 11

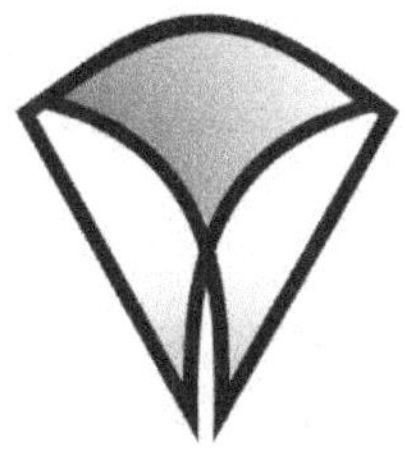

Uncle Mike was brewing a cup of coffee in the Keurig that Jonathan brought for Alessandra, a coffee drinker. Of course, it collected dust in the years it's been there, but it was exciting to see it used for once in the five years since he brought it down.

Alessandra wasn't familiar with the unusual and uncertain material blend that insulated the armory. It seemed like a steel-infused polymer of some sort that looked like the tavern wall, glistening in specks of white like a dark grayish metallic mauve. The armory was about ten yards from where they were sitting, covered in a clear plastic coating that almost looked like something you would see at the skating rink at the park she used to visit in Houston.

At the end of the armory based, she saw different suits and wicked outfits set up on mannequins that seemed to match her dimensions marked with the same symbols she saw in her dreams. The polymer material was also part of the outfits but in various colors. Some were a soft pink, some a soft blue, and her favorite ones were in a muted mauve. She had been part of the Fashion Design course at the Academy of Design and Technology. She bailed from the University of Incarnate Word after having her entire college experience ruined by the unfairness of systematic and institutional racism, which had the school protecting the prized college football quarterback. She dropped out.

She pursued her education at a technical school, which never got her the dream job they promised her. The football player had so many issues, which Alessandra thought, *maybe that is why he is the way he was. Poor little lamb, stuck with his daddy and mommy issues. Maybe if he got the help he needed, maybe if he wasn't an asshole.*"

"He was a lost cause and a total asshole Babe," Jonathan chimed in.

"JONATHAN!" she yelled. "Can you stay out of my head, please; this is all fucken new and freaky for me," she replied, annoyed.

"Sorry Babe, I can't help it. It happens when you feel anger," he said apologetically.

"WHAT?" she said in a whirl. "So, wait; is that why you…"

"…You guys have all the awesome things in this era," Uncle Mike said amusingly.

Tia turned around at the steal chair and the steal table that looked like a surgical platform and said, "Wait, you don't know what a Keurig is?" she asked, dumbfounded. "Where have you been then?" she asked confusedly.

"Give her a tour of the armory, Jonathan Carlos; let me make a cup for our Warrior Princess here," he said in sternness. "Would you like one?" he asked kindly.

"Can you make it how Abuela can?" he said.

"Of course, but Jonathan, move for a bit," he signaled while he snuck up on Alessandra as this place amazed her.

"MIJA!" Uncle Mike screamed, holding her steady and seeing Alessandra burst into the bright light flipping the table she was facing, putting her crossed arms down, seeing the table go with force toward the plastic border, going into a dark abyss and floating for a few seconds, and watching it return to the original table entirely back where it originally sat.

She looked at Jonathan and then looked at her Uncle Mike and then back to the plastic proctor in amazement. She said in shock, "Damn, I should have paid attention to my quantum physics professor.

Jonathan said in joyful pride, "Welcome to your destiny, Babe."

She smiled while turning to Uncle Mike and then to Jonathan, seeing his excited face light up. "Damn, Xena Warrior Princess and Wonder Woman have nothing on this hood rat.

"Mija, really," Uncle Mike scolded.

"Hey, I know my place. I took it like a champ when those basic bitches at my job in Houston tried to insult me," she shrugged.

"You're better than that and much more prestigious than you give yourself credit for," he corrected.

"Well," she shrugged. "I am hood rat who's going to fuck shit up for evil scum bags now," she said proudly. "But one question."

Uncle Mike and Jonathan answered in a concerning manner in unison, "Yeah?"

"Are those outfits for me?" she asked curiously.

"Yeah, Babe, I picked them out. I hope you like them," Jonathan answered in uncertainty.

Alessandra jumped up to kiss a now smiling Jonathan, wrapping her arms around his strong, broad shoulders. She turned to Uncle Mike and screamed, "COMICON, here we come."

Uncle Mike slapped his hand on his forehead, saying in frustration, "Aye, Este Niña.

"Tio, I'm kidding," she said amusingly.

"Jonathan, take her on the tour before she kills me in this lifetime," he shooed while waving his hands away in frustration.

"Yes, sir," he said affirmatively.

"And Jonathan," he requested.

"Yes, sir."

"You're part of the family now. Call me Tio."

Jonathan looked back and smiled with a peaceful smile, saying, "Yes, Tio."

After the quick tour of the armory and the assault closet, Uncle Mike looked a little perplexed as he looked at Alessandra with the what's wrong now face he gave to Jonathan.

Jonathan looked at him with his I don't know the face.

"What are you not telling me now," she asked suspiciously.

"Nothing, Babe," he said in suspicion, seeing Alessandra flaunt her disapproving look of dismay.

Alessandra turned to look at her Uncle as he spoke up. "We are curious why you have that thinking face like Cher on *Clueless* has all the time."

"Awww, thanks, Tio, for you saying something. I don't want to be in the doghouse tonight," Jonathan said in relief.

"You all didn't hear me this time," she asked, surprised.

"Wha.... "Jonathan asked.

"...Yeah, I figured out how to control that since you didn't let me get a word in during the entire sure Charming," she said jokingly. She thought to herself, *Ha, mother fu...* as Uncle Mike interrupted vocally.

"That mouth, ma'am."

Alessandra thought to herself, *That's what I get for being arrogant.*

"You're not arrogant. You're trying to teach them, Babe," Jonathan vocalized reassuringly.

"Thanks for having my back, Babe," she said lovingly.

"Can you tell what's on your mind and quit the shenanigans before you make me throw up in my mouth," Uncle Mike said in disgust.

Alessandra turned around with a grin, "You say that now.

"Just out with-it, Hun, before I drop dead again," Uncle Mike said.

"Well, I just thought this puts Batman and Miles from *Spiderman* to shame. But wait, that can happen."

"When did you take things so literally," he said in disappointment, slapping his head on his forehead again.

"Yeah, Babe, I mean, we know your Warrior royalty but stop acting like a Kardashian," Jonathan said jokingly.

"Shut up, Jonathan," Uncle Mike and Alessandra chimed.

"Sorry," Jonathan smirked as he shrugged. "Now I know where she gets it from. It all makes sense." He made the head explosion gesture.

Alessandra just laughed. "Now you see why I love that guy so much."

Uncle Mike said after his chuckle, which turned immediately serious, "So are you ready to train harder than you ever have?"

"Are we sparing, Tio?" Alessandra said in delight.

"Let's see if your dreams match the real deal," Uncle Mike said as he gestured that Neo gesture that Keanu Reeves did in *The Matrix*.

"Only on one condition Tio Mike," she said in seriousness.

"What's that," he asked sternly.

"We need some jams," she yelled. "DJ, play my song," she requested as Jonathan pulled out his phone.

"You got it, Babe," he said as he played Jennifer Lopez's *Waiting for Tonight*.

She looked at him with a disappointed face, saying, "Not that one.

"Oh, the ANYTHING FOR SALINAS song," as he mocked the chulo characters from the *Selena* movie.

"Babe, really," she said in disappointment. "Let's not insult the Queen of Tejano by saying that. Let's call it by its correct title *Last Dance Disco Medley*, she demanded.

As Jonathan searched for the song, he said, "You got it, Warrior Princess," and played *Last Dance Disco Medley;* the high tempo version.

"Alright, Tio, let's head to the sparing rink," as she happily pointed to the plastic-covered area in the middle of the armory.

Uncle Mike looked at Jonathan with an amused face and looked immediately at Alessandra, who was now facing him with the we are doing this look as he said, "ANYTHING FOR SALINAS," in the same cholo tone.

Alessandra looked at Jonathan attempting to look serious while holding in the laughter, and then at Uncle Mike, who couldn't keep his laughter in, saying in disappointment, "You guys are assholes."

Jonathan couldn't hold the laugher anymore, and trying to mimic the nineties commercial, said, "I did it by watching you."

Alessandra looked at him in disappointment, which didn't contain his laughter saying, "You're lucky I love you, fine ass."

Chapter 12

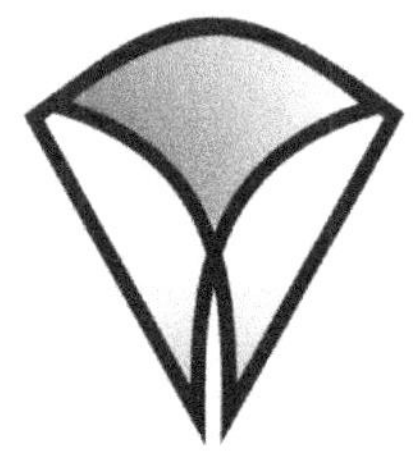

Training began with a refresher of the ballistic combats training Uncle Mike taught her at age fifteen, along with the mixed martial arts training shortly after. She was extremely rusty but caught up pretty quickly.

Uncle Mike was six foot four with a mestizo brown complexion. His sculpted face had a narrow, broad nose with a strong jawline that resembled Adam Levine's with a similar five o'clock shadow. He's stocky but muscular and wore his signature USCM shirt that Jonathan wanted to keep when they were helping. She thought about the ugly things she said to him when she thought he threw it away, thinking, *Damn, I was a bitch that day.*

Abuela got rid of some remaining clothes after the burial, which now she questioned. She looked at Jonathan, hoping he would hear what she was about to say next. He grinned, and she shook her head while saying, "Damn, I can't see Adam Levine the same way anymore. Ewwww, a little pervy now."

"Yes, it is Mija," Uncle Mike said, scolding. "He's a rocket scientist who helped us prepare for your role here in this solar system star cluster."

"Wow, I knew that guy was super smart," she said in assuring amazement.

"He is a little arrogant. But the 'at ease disease' tactic helped him get humble quick like it did a young Warrior Princess long ago," he said in affirmation as he grinned.

"Yes, Tio, I know. I was a little shit for a while," she said in disappointment.

"Well?"

Jonathan stood between the protective covering, which was later a time continuum that reverted everything to normal. She mesmerized him in amazement with the progress she had quickly made as he whispered to himself, "Damn, she's incredible."

Alessandra fell to the ground with a hard and quick roundhouse that Uncle Mike executed, which had her thump in force to the ground.

"AGAIN ALESSANDRA," he demanded.

She remained still for a few seconds while she tried to recover from the powerful fall.

"Recover quicker," Uncle Mike demanded. "You only have a split second before your ass becomes grass," he said in a stern, firm tone.

She got up, shaking off the pain, and thought, *I can do this,"* which immediately resulted in an aqua glow as she felt her body recover.

Jonathan jumped in glee as he yelled in joy, "She got her other powers!"

"The body only recovers in a humbled spirit," Uncle Mike said proudly.

She positioned herself in a crane-like fighting stance and did the Neo signal as she grinned in seriousness.

"Don't forget the scientific theories, Babe," Jonathan yelled.

Uncle Mike jumped up like Neo in the matrix as he jumped six feet in the delivery of an air running kick assault.

"Professor Longoria would be proud of me if she remembered the things, I remembered." She attempted to deflect the attack with a back roll, which resulted in a stern backflip that ended up hitting Uncle Mike in the face.

"That's my future wifey," Jonathan shouted, jumping for joy as he followed with "WOOOOOHHHH."

Uncle Mike hit the ground hard with a thud as Alessandra landed gracefully like a Power Ranger on both feet.

Uncle Mike got up quickly and applauded his niece, saying with pride, "Well done, Mija. I expected you to be well off the wagon on training," as he continued to celebrate.

"Thanks, Tio," she said in proud grace.

"Ready to work on tapping into the superpowers," he asked anxiously.

"Yeah, the healing or the jumping," she asked in a focused manner.

"Let's start with your physical ones and then with the weapons."

"Wait, there are more than the ones I know about?" she asked excitedly. She looked at Jonathan with his grin-to-grin smile. He had the same look when she finally agreed to marry him.

He nodded in delight and said, "Yes, Babe. You're like the real-life wonder woman without the fancy things," he said in delight.

"Let's not insult Gal Gadot. She's awesome and pretty and probably the only girl I'd switch teams for if you pissed me off," she said thoughtfully.

"That will never happen, but I'd pay to see that," he said jokingly.

"Shut up, Star Boy," Uncle Mike and Alessandra yelled in disapproval.

Jonathan just shrugged his shoulders and grinned as he lifted his eyebrows, thinking slightly of the idea when Alessandra's quick rebuttal interrupted him.

"You know I can call the whole thing off and give you this ring back," she added.

Uncle Mike looked at Alessandra with a surprised look as he said in shock, "You heard him, damn Mija, that's not supposed to happen until you mastered your armory training," he said in amazement.

"She's AP grade," Jonathan said proudly.

"Can we get on with this, Tio and Babe," she said eagerly. Before they could speak, Alessandra said, "Don't do the Salinas thing. You're going to make me automatically blow up this city as I also hear your thoughts, Tio."

Jonathan and Uncle Mike looked at each other.

Uncle Mike turned to Alessandra and replied, "Yes, Ma'am."

"Don't piss her off, Tio. She's on fire," Jonathan said in a loud whisper.

"Okay, Alessandra, this is where you have to use your emotions to tap into my emotions as each emotion will release a power."

"She's a powerhouse," Uncle Mike warned! "Get in your fighting stance," he demanded sternly.

She followed the order and positioned herself back in her usual stance. "So, is that mind-reading thing evoked by my confusion?"

Uncle Mike nodded with a smile. "The Universe provides the answers when you're lost in the world," he reassured. "We just don't see the signs. This is the world now tapping into the things you need to survive. Now focus on the times fear overran your life," he said, moving away from the expected blast as he circled the sparring arena. He moved toward her direction.

She held her stance as she thought about when her mother's unconfirmed boyfriend touched her at four years old and felt a heat developing within her. She saw the amber glow reveal itself to her as she saw her left arm glowing.

"The atoms in your body are an advanced form, more like an evolved form of what the normal human body has. Formaldehyde, mercury, and all the world's common pollutants in the air particles are infused with the atoms' molecular structure in your body. The water we drink and even the food a Milky Way Solar System Earth being has in their body normally makes you prone to cancers. The potassium, neon, and magnesium binders that wrap around your cell with an extragalactic element called Turiorion is what protects you. It enhances your senses, and even gives you your superhuman power," Jonathan said in scholarly pride.

"What the fuck? I'm an alien then," Alessandra said as she saw the glow slowly fade.

"Focus, Alessandra," Uncle Mike corrected slowly.

She thought of that night and saw the glow return. "So, is that what you have?" she asked Jonathan as she held her glow steady, getting stronger?

"Don't be silly, Babe, I am not Turiorion," he corrected. "I am Azulian. The Azulionon of the binder in my molecular structure. It has the same base that you have just bound by a different element," he repeated in the same corrective scholarly tone.

"He's from another dimension, which is a mirroring image from another time," Uncle Mike said in assurance. "He and I had our differences, which has a better Latin heritage which we have in this world. Jonathan Carlos is more knowledgeable about this. Keep focusing and think of the day you fought back against your attacker," he chided.

She thought of that day, and the blast of energy jolted out as it did in her dream. She had to secure herself from the power protruding as she saw the energy getting absorbed into the transparent protective wall.

"Thanks, Tio," Jonathan said thankfully. "So, you have various powers that include a Turiorion blast. When deflected, the blast will absorb back, making your blast mimic a radioactive atomic bomb. When focused, it can contain the blast as matter and recycle back as normal elements found in the world you're in. Your telekinetic power is like a side effect of that. Think of it like a radio frequency finding static neurons in the air. You can manipulate the time and matter in your existing world," he added as he educated her with an educational tone.

"It's the... "Alessandra interrupted.

It's the "Time, Matter, and Space Theory," she said in fascination and shock.

"Damn Babe, Professor Longoria would sure be proud right about now," as he nodded and clapped in prideful content.

"Okay, Alessandra. Now think of the victory that you felt that day," Uncle Mike added.

She saw the ray of energy floating in what looked like a star system in the background, which looked like a pixilated cluster of what appeared to be the shape of atoms. She kept her stance as she remembered the day; she told her maternal Abuela Maria what happened that day. The feeling she had was pride and security as she felt safe for the first time in her short life. She saw the pixilated atoms return to the ray of light, its original form. It started slowly, and then it rushed as she popped her chest back and felt it enter her body. She looked at both hands spread down to her sides, turning from yellow to hot pink.

Uncle Mike pulled out the concealed apple he had hidden in his jogging pants and threw the apple in the air, and said, "Jonathan, could you help me out?"

Jonathan replied, "Sure thing," as he focused on the apple, which now moved in slow motion, ready to fall from its original velocity.

Uncle Mike looked at Alessandra as she looked at him and said, "Focus on the apple," which followed with her looking back at the apple. "Derrick," which was her attacker in college.

Her face turned to rage as she protruded a hot pink bolt of atomic energy that began in slow-motion to reach the apple as it slowed, exposing the ball of pink energy in the apple.

"Now, think of your place and comfort."

She thought about Jonathan and the times he was there for her. The apple turned to dust as Jonathan stopped the space manipulation. Uncle Mike and Jonathan looked at each other and looked at Alessandra. Jonathan yelled as he continuously jumped in excitement.

Alessandra looked at the dust on the floor in shock, saying, "No fucken way."

Uncle Mike walked to Alessandra to ease her shock. As she looked at her Uncle in the face, Uncle Mike responded in amusement, "You're not a ticking time bomb anymore."

Chapter 13

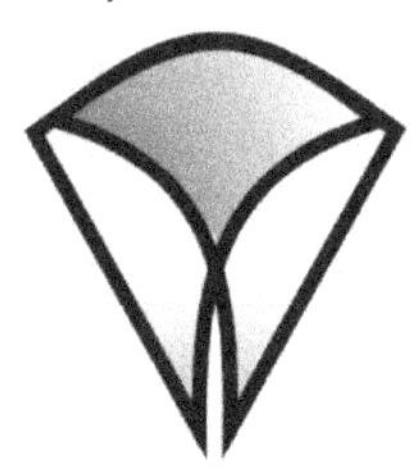

"So, who is this pageant reject in my dream," Alessandra said in a regarding tone as she took a bite of her Salata mandarin salad?

"That is Mictlantecuhtli," Uncle Mike said before Alessandra chimed in.

"The Aztec God of Death," she said in alarm.

"You remember your Latin history," Uncle Mike said in amazement.

She heard the echoing of splashing of water from the waterfall entrance. She listened to the rhythmic footsteps of Jonathan's distressed 1965 Converse echoing as he made his way into the private armory that only celestial beings and decedents could access.

He walked to the right side of the table where Alessandra was wearing his signature wearing a cerulean shirt they purchased at the San Marcos outlet after watching *The Devil Wears Prada,* which Alessandra insisted needed to be Prada. Alessandra thought to herself,

"For sixty bucks thanks to the eighty percent of sale was a steal."

He walked to Alessandra and leaned in with a kiss. "It was a steal," he said as he looked at her, lovingly, and proudly.

"Aw, come on, guys. Get a room already. " He flashed the garment bag that had the label of her failed attempt to launch her fashion line that read "Libredad."

"I brought that amazing dress you wore at the fashion show at the Academy when you took your last walk as a featured designer," Jonathan said as he raised his eyebrows repeatedly. He added in pride.

"The one that everyone called me a poser for using mauve and a studded empire waist leather embellishment," she added in embarrassment. She looked up and smiled, thinking about her inspiration for the garment. It was the time that they cruised down to the Hill Country to visit the secluded lake her mom and dad found as teenagers. They took her there after learning how to swim to celebrate her victory, followed by a subtle golden neon glow that she started forming from on her arms, glimmering a yellow green color. "The one I used Aerosmith's music that helped me create the entire line," she added.

"Yeah, it only suited you. It reminds me of that bad-ass shooting game 'Revolution X' that going to the missions had you talk about your happy moments in childhood when your Tio and Dad took you to the arcade," he confirmed. He looked in space for a moment, thinking about the game.

"You obsessed over that game for a good five months," she said amusingly.

He remained staring up in space, thinking about the play-by-play of the game and his new profound love for the band as he said in a whisper, "That game was fucken badass."

"Kids can we stay focus," Uncle Mike commanded.

"Sorry, Tio, what did I miss?" as Jonathan came back to his current Earth.

"So, I got our Warrior Princess caught up with Mictlantecuhtli and was about to go into what his intentions are in this realm," he added in acerbity.

He made a disgusted face as he said in antipathy as he said, "I fucken hate that guy."

"Okay, so pageant reject is the Aztec God of Death, so can we continue with the four-one-one," she asserted.

Jonathan continued, "So this douche bag is here to unleash his legion of the dead by the social act of cultural zombification," he said in earnestness.

"So, the theory that I have that I feel people are becoming narcissistic," she said in assuredness.

"Yeah, which is being used by Revolution," he said in loathing.

"Wait, so why are you working for those assholes?" she asked in animosity.

"He's not working for them. He's infiltrating," in affirmation.

"Really Babe, come on, give me more credit than that," he said in dismay. He continued to explain the purpose of his presence. "We have been on them as they petrified an entire planet. It was a faraway planet in the same plane that mirrors this existing one. Uncle Mike is our celestial Ballistics Generalissimo. He earned that rank by the active energy he exerted after his death; he used to be a spy. His ghost recon tactics allowed him to regain his physical being but in a different realm and Galaxy. He successfully infiltrated the attacks in Celestron, the sister realm, to your existing realm. Mictlantecuhtli could not fully identify his essence. Mictlantecuhtli senses him but could not physically recognize him. That is why he attacked this realm and planet. He knew who he was since in his moment of the grief of not being able to be with you physically; he could sense your essence which had him come here," he added as he was recapping her in seriousness.

"Thanks, Tio," she said jokingly.

"It was heartbreaking not to be with you, knowing I could travel in all celestial realms and not be able to protect you. Seeing you in a moment of trouble that night in college broke my heart," he said as he reached and put his hand on top of hers.

She looked at him with tears falling down his face.

"My so-called spidcy-senses came in that night. I came here after helping a child when I was a child from getting human trafficked."

"This world's social service system took action by covering up a situation that made them look like know-it-all assholes," he said in apprehension.

"It wasn't until I was fighting him directly that he found out who you were," Uncle Mike said in disgust.

"Tio, it's not your fault; I understand," Alessandra confirmed.

"So, they had him come here prematurely the Celestial Organization intervene and have Tio here come to aid the infiltration," Jonathan added.

"So, what are we in for?" Alessandra added in concern.

Uncle Mike sighed as he replied, "We are unsure." Jonathan chimed in.

"What we know," he emphasized as he looked at Uncle Mike with a stern face. "Is that he is assuming the identity of 'Antonio Castillo,' the CEO of the show Mi Gente. He has two casting calls. One for 'Mi Gente' and one for the Adult Film Company called 'Seven,' which is an acronym for…"

Alessandra interrupted, "…The Seven Deadly Sins," in alarm.

Uncle Mike looked at Alessandra in amazement as he said, "Damn. Sunday School didn't fail you, huh," he said contently.

"Well, you know Abuela," she said as she shrugged. "She follows the Catholic religion, she instills values, but always rationally separates the good and enforces that, and he divides the bad that enables those behaviors," she said in content.

"You got to love Mom," Uncle Mike said in contentment with a grin.

"Speaking of Abuela, you need to call her," Jonathan added.

"Was she worried?" she asked in concern.

He smiled, making his eyebrow gesture as he said, "No. She knew you were with your hunk a burning love and knew you were safe," he said amusement.

"Wait, how did you get there?" she asked in a regarding manner.

"One power Jonathan has is he can materialize inorganic particles," Uncle Mike said scholastically.

"Which gives him the ability to materialize atoms that are non-living," she replied as both of the guys looked at her in shock.

She looked at both of the men in her genuine expression, and she said, "What?! I know stuff," she said.

"Okay, Sabrina from *Charlie Angels,"* Jonathan said in amusement.

Alessandra shrugged her shoulders.

"Let's take her to the artillery area so she can pick her weapons," Uncle Mike said as he got up from his seat.

"Fuck yeah," Jonathan said as he helped Alessandra, extending his arm like Leonardo DiCaprio in *Titanic.*

Alessandra thought about the game she and Jonathan enjoyed that night before they almost broke up when the tropical storm turn hurricane for the Gulf Coast turned into Katrina. She looked back at the phone with a spooked face as Aerosmith's *Sweet Emotions* tuned in. "What the fuck?" she said in shock.

Jonathan and Uncle Mike both looked at one another with a shocked face.

"Holy shit, she gained her other power," Jonathan said in surprise.

"What's that? she asked," still in shock.

"You gained the ability to manipulate inorganic radioactive frequencies," Uncle Mike said.

Jonathan took out his phone and tapped his phone, which caused Alessandra to look at him in confusion.

"Babe, we already have tunes," Alessandra said in confusion.

He put his phone away as he said, "I'm marrying a badass." He kissed her on the lips as he escorted her to catch up with the pace her Uncle Mike excreted.

"Who said diamonds were a girl's best friend," she said as they walked side by side next to Uncle Mike.

"Do you know that I helped Elizabeth Banks come up with that story plot," Uncle Mike added in his usual sternness?

Chapter 14

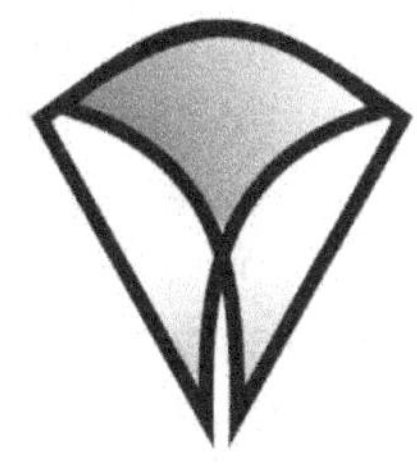

It was 6:45 p.m. when they arrived at the hotel. Alessandra was lying in bed before the live audition segment of Mi Gente. The sounds of the shower sprits fell on the floor of Jonathan's shower. She flipped over to lie on her stomach, which followed a tug to pull the kimono belt that got stuck between the mattress and the platform.

Jonathan's off-tune singing echoed the lyrics of *Sweet Emotion.* Alessandra threw her head into the pillow and thought in a cumbersome manner. She heard the shower stop, which had her pick up her head from the pillow as she whispered, "Fuck" thinking *I bet you he's prepping for his pep talk.*

Jonathan opened the door in sternness as he replied, "Yes, I'm giving you the damn pep talk as he walked toward Alessandra.

"Babe, this shit I'm forced to deal with is real. It's fucken major," she said in a panic.

He walked over to where she laid in a stomping gesture and kneeled as close as he could to her with an empathic face as he replied, "I get it."

"Babe, the whole fate of San Antonio is in my hands. What if I fail?" she said in despair. An aqua glow started; she didn't notice as she looked down, closing her eyes holding back tears.

Jonathan noticed, trying not to hide his surprise as he said in attempted empathy, focusing on her face, "Babe, you're not."

Alessandra flipped over in anger, having her hair fall over her left shoulder, replying, "Oh. Really? You think I am going to fuck up too," she added in disappointment.

In defense, Jonathan got up, exposing his completely naked body as his genital swung like a wind chime in the wind. "Oh, here we go again. The pitiful Alessandra feels sorry for herself" in disappointment as he focused on the time and space around them subliminally.

Alessandra bolted up from the bed, having her hot pink printed flower kimono she wore move majestically like a man of war in water. "You always do this shit. You always undermine my strengths, and you always glorify my vulnerabilities," as she bolted to the bathroom door.

Jonathan stopped her in her steps in the foot-wide space between the bed and the television. "You're not doing this shit today, Alessandra," as he stepped forward.

Alessandra sat on the ledge in the middle of the bed.

"You will not swing from the chandelier today," he affirmed as he took a step back in caution. He could see

Alessandra glowing from aqua to dark neon green, still focusing on the time and space subliminally.

"I fucken hate it when you do this. I hate this. I hate you," Alessandra cried.

He thought about the possibilities that may have happened. Jonathan kneeled in front of her as he embraced her in mournful tears. "You will not lose me, Alessandra. You will not lose Tio either. I mean, he has to return, but we can visit him," he said comfortingly.

"I figured it was too good to be true. But I can't lose you. What if I do something wrong or put you in danger? I know you can't be there always. And I know you're always there to rescue me, which explains why you always have impeccable timing. What if I put you in danger?" she said violently, sobbing. "What if I get you killed?" she said, crying harder. "I haven't even told you thanks for rescuing me all those times," she continued mournfully. "I didn't even tell you how happy I am to be the future, Mrs. King," she said in the same manner. "I haven't told you enough times how much I love you," which had her cover her face as she wept.

Jonathan smiled in admiration and softness as he gently pulled her hands away as he brushed her hair out of her face and wiped the tears falling on the left cheek. She looked back as he said in a delicate and sultry voice, "Nothing is going to happen, Princess; I promise."

Her cry weakened as she stared into his ocean blue eyes and whispered, "I love you so much, Charming."

Jonathan looked deep into her now sunset brown eyes and said sultrily soft, "I love you too," as he went in for a kiss.

The kiss started with pecks and began to progress slowly as they both stood up as Jonathan untied the robe tie as he pulled it off, falling to the floor like a feather. The kiss intensified with more demanding kisses as he laid her gently onto the bed and caressed her soft olive skin. He stopped for a moment and looked at one another as the song from The Weeknd, *Earned It,* came to mind as it played from both their phones in unison.

"You see how amazingly powerful you are, Babe," he said delicately, reassuring as he continued the kiss as he entered her, which followed with a delicate moan. He kissed her as he gently thrust between her plump thighs, which made her release a louder moan. He flipped her over, having her in a sitting position, still embracing her soft body as he gently looked at her, which made her climax.

"Don't stop, Charming," she said as he thrust harder.

He gave her pleasure as he thrust gently but with a light force as he expressed a face of blissful contentment. "You're my person, Mi Amor," he said as he continued. He flipped her back on her back gently as he kissed her again, being body to body. She continued the kiss with a whispered moaning.

Alessandra gently pulled back and said in bliss, "You okay?" which had Jonathan continue the tempo.

His face showed signs of climax as he sped the tempo, whispering, "I love Babe. You're always going to be my person," and kissed her as he gave a pleasurable and thankful moan, which had Alessandra climax and followed his lead. The thrust slowed down as his body quivered along with Alessandra. They came to a stop as he laid on top of Alessandra, still intertwined as he looked at her with a loving and appreciative look that had him steal a kiss from her again as she smiled.

"I love you, Babe, and nothing will happen," he reassured her in a delicate whisper.

"I don't know what I would do without you, Charming," she said in the same delicate and loving tone.

"Ride and die, Babe. Ride and die," he said in a comforting whisper.

Alessandra thought about the last words he said after they parted on the last kiss before leaving for Los Angeles. The song that played, *Earned It*, stopped playing and followed with their song from that final moment in their hometown, David Guetta, and Ushers *Without You*, as they kissed once again.

They lost themselves in a long, embraced moment as they heard the door slam. They heard "The package is here."

"Oh shit!" in hesitation followed by a panicked, "I'm sorry Mr. King" as the bellboy turned away and left the puffed package at the entrance table as he hurried out the door.

They looked at each other laughing.

"Wouldn't be my first audience now, would it?" Alessandra said.

Jonathan got up to retrieve the package. He opened it and returned to bed. Jonathan unfolded what looked like two graphic tees. "What pendejada did you do?" He sat his naked body on the bed and revealed the shirts.

Alessandra showed a blissful and content look, thinking, *This is why I'm marrying him.*

"Me too, Babe. Remember when you asked me what I was doing on my phone during training," he said excitedly. "Well, this was it," he said proudly.

The hotel phone rang, and Jonathan picked it up, and said, "Okay, tell him to give us thirty minutes," and hung up.

"It's showtime, Babe. Let's turn Mictlantecuhtli's ass into grass," he said, mocking Uncle Mike.

She chuckled and replied, "His ass is grass, which isn't appropriate in this situation."

"Eh, he'll get over it," Jonathan said as he put the shirt down. He grabbed Alessandra by the hand and mocked Jack Dawson from Titanic as he said, "But first showers."

Alessandra nodded in confirmation as he scooped her up. She playfully screamed, and he put her down for a brief second. She looked at him, concerned, "What's wrong, Babe."

He rushed back to bed to straighten out the first shirt. It said, "I'm marrying a badass. He's my badass." Next, he unfolded and flattened the second shirt. The second shirt that he laid said, "I'm marrying a badass. She's my badass and my person."

Jonathan then picked up his soon to be bride saying, "Our shower awaits, shall we, Mrs. King."

Chapter 15

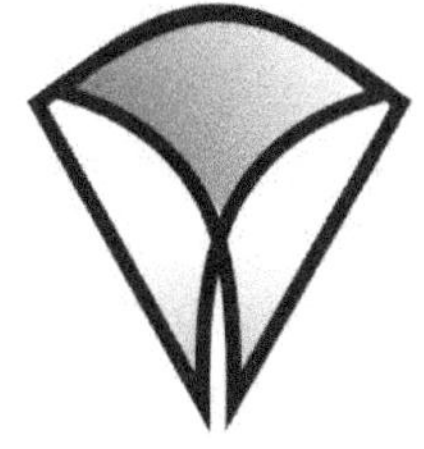

It was 8:30 p.m, when Uncle Mike pulled up at the Hotel Emma. He was in the valet section's designated parking as he waited for the soon to be married couple to come down.

"Come on, Carlos," he said as he glanced at the clock and pulled down the mirror to situate his collar and adjust the top hat he wore to fit the role of a Passeio driver asked himself out loud, "Does this open?" As he located the roof button, it startled him when the automatic movement of the moon roof opened. "Damn, that's fancy," he said humorously. He looked at the starry night sky and took in the breezy air that blew in from the top of the moon roof and stared. "It's good to be back." He heard in the distance the loud laugh of Alessandra joking with Jonathan coming around the corner.

Jonathan was wearing a navy tuxedo suit with a sky-blue button-up with a dusty mauve tie to match Alessandra's outfit with black leather dress shoes shined to perfection.

Uncle Mike opened the car and stepped out in black slacks, a black sports jacket, and sporting his top hat. "If I'm going to play the part, let's make sure we don't do this half-ass," he assured himself. Uncle Mike went toward the passenger side to open the vehicle's back door.

"Tio. Hey!" Jonathan said as he sped further to speed up to greet Uncle Mike.

Uncle Mike was breath taken as she approached when the background music played Berlin's *Take My Breath Away*. Tears fell from Uncle Mike's eyes.

"She looks stunning, doesn't she?" Jonathan said in a whisper.

"That's my baby girl," Uncle Mike said, holding back tears. He engaged with the hotel staff. He watched her shaking hands and embracing them. "Thank you for everything you guys have done and the hospitality you have shown." Alessandra engaged with every single person and expressed their gratitude humbly.

"Keep her safe, Jonathan, please, son."

"I respect the Romero family creed, sir. My life before her, sir," he said as he looked at him with a reassuring smile.

Alessandra was wearing an artistically pleated strapless mauve metallic brocade dress. The dress mimicked a Japanese printed dress that glistened metallic rose gold with the same mauve overskirt. Alessandra's dress started high and draped low, fluttering in the wind of her walk as she walked toward her two favorite guys in the world. She wore her hair in a flowing twist that draped her right shoulder, exposing what looked like rhinestone dog tags she had confiscated, and Jonathan molded and replicated to make it a semi-precious metal. The leather belt studded in spikes held the underskirt that hugged her curves and slightly flared, making it vintage. She wore the rose gold heels she despised her Uncle Mike got for her to look more ladylike during high school graduation. That made Uncle Mike tear up more. She didn't notice as she embraced in a similar look that Jonathan had but was slightly different. Jonathan's look resembled the proud face of a future husband. "Okay, that's just coincidence this time, not me," she said as she turned to look at him and now becoming concerned by Uncle Mike's look.

Uncle Mike immediately replied as he said, "You look amazing, baby girl."

Alessandra's concerned look turned into an empathctic and comforting face and she brushed the tears off her and Tio's face.

"I can change it something else now that I mastered that gift today," she said empathetically.

"No," her uncle said, "it's the perfect song."

Jonathan added, "And she designed the dress Tio."

Uncle Mike couldn't hold back the tears as the guilt that plagued him settled in as he cried, "I wish I were physically there."

Jonathan was going to say something as she said in perfect unison with Jonathan as she whimpered, "You were there in spirit." Alessandra also had tears fall as she hugged her Uncle Mike in a hard and a reunited embrace as they cried.

Jonathan felt his eyes puff in redness and develop tears. He noticed that an audience formed as he sniffled his tears back in and directed the crowd. Mesmerizing those who assumed it was a father and daughter reunion, they knew the person Jonathan was. The pedestrians were unaware of what going on as they whispered negative suspicions as he yelled, "Alright, everyone, nothing to see here. Just a father-daughter reunion. Can you give us some privacy here please?"

Those who thought negatively tried to hide their suspicions as they began deleting the pictures they took.

Jonathan headed into the crowd demanding people with phones hand them over for inspections and shaking hands with the staff as he thanked them for their services.

Alessandra and Uncle Mike broke their embrace and giggled, still in their tears. Alessandra then went to assist him in quality control.

Uncle Mike whispered under his breath as he heard the comments and the descriptive rudeness of those invading their privacy. They were voyeurs, and he demanded an apology, which they offered, saying, "They make an excellent team."

Jonathan and Alessandra walked back hand in hand. He extended his hand for Alessandra to enter the car; he closed the door as Alessandra stared in space to get emotionally ready for the night.

Uncle Mike extended his hand as Jonathan looked down at his and then up at Uncle Mike, smiling in the proud affirmation that embraced in a firm handshake and a quick firm hug. As he slowly wrapped his arms around Uncle Mike, Jonathan, confused for a moment, said, "You're not a hugger, sir. Everything fine?"

Uncle Mike broke the hug immediately and gave Jonathan one final firm stare, “I’m proud to have you in the family, son. Thank you for taking care of her for me,” he said, holding back tears again in his attempted seriousness.

Jonathan smiled in a peaceful affirmative stare and replied, “Anything for my person and our family.”

Chapter 16

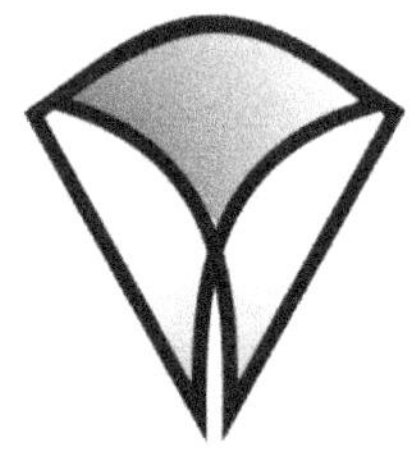

They were fifteen minutes away from the studio. There was a parade of cars stopped. There was only one way they could get into the studio's entrance, so they waited in the line of vehicles.

"Seems like it's a good turnout, huh, Charming?" Alessandra said in confirmation. "I hope you're dying tonight is in the program," she said jokingly.

"Alessandra," Uncle Mike scolded.

"I'm kidding, Tio," she said. "So, what can we expect tonight," she said in seriousness.

"What are your weapons of choice?" Uncle Mike affirmed.

In a mimicked sternness, "Well sir, Alessandra has her oldie but goodie choices, the long Sai and Kitana blade that she has holstered on her thighs. The Sai is on the underneath of the spiked belt for dramatized effect. The Kitana as its retractable is on her right side," he confirmed.

Alessandra and Uncle Mike both looked at him with an insulted face.

"What?" Jonathan, said in the same offended tone, as he shrugged his shoulders. "I like the way Tio says it, so official," he said in defense.

Uncle Mike proudly smiled and said, "Thank you."

"We didn't train with these, Alessandra," he said in concern. "Think you can handle it?"

"I got this, Tio," she assured. "Jonathan and I spared one time during the pussy-ass tae-bo class we took at the over-glorified boxing gym that had us kicked out cause the gym members were asking if we did personal training."

"Carlos… I mean Jonathan, what do you think, son?" he asked in an unsettling tone.

"Tio, no, she has this down pack like her cooking skills," he said confidently.

"You cook, Alessandra?" Uncle Mike asked shockingly.

"She's terrific, Tio; she makes the best Carne guisada and the best Arroz con glandule's." His stomach growled. "She's the reason I had to double up the workouts," he said teasingly. "Her tortilla making skills. Not so much," he said teasingly.

Alessandra looked at him in discontent and smiled humbly. "Yeah, Tio. I just don't have the patience to practice perfecting the art of rolling that well. It's a waste of time," she said in annoyance as she thought about the tedious task.

"That's what a tortilla presser is for," he added in a disgraced and confused way.

Alessandra and Jonathan paused as they secured the armory to her body and looked at him in disappointment.

"What?" Uncle Mike said in embarrassment.

Alessandra said in disappointment, "How dare you."

Jonathan replied in smugness, "Yeah, Tio, it's a disgrace to say that kind of thing here, sir, with all due respect."

"Tortilla snobs surround me," he said in a disgusting entitlement. "I blame mom for that mother…"

Alessandra responded with a sharp, "Shut your mouth."

"Yeah, Tio, let's not talk about Abuela like that. That's rude and insulting," Jonathan added, nodding his head in disappointment.

He grinned as he replied, "At least you guys haven't lost the art of respect."

Jonathan nodded in additional disappointment and said, "Are you calling us entitled?"

"Basta, Jonathan, please. We're getting personal, and I still need to be as ready as I can be," Alessandra said in annoyance.

"Yes, Babe," he added in conformity.

"Okay, you got the weapons part down. You think you got your combat training down?" Uncle Mike asked in a confirming tone.

"Yes, I might be a few moves off, but I can deflect attacks very well," she added.

"Carl… Jonathan," he asked for confirmation.

"Yeah, she's the master of deflecting," he said in a joking undertone.

Alessandra looked at him with a resting bitch face.

"How about the powers?" Uncle Mike asked.

"I know how to stop in and engage it mostly," she confirmed. "If I want to shine like a ray of light, I think of

Derek. If I want to stop it, I think of Jonathan," she confirmed as she lovingly smiled at Jonathan.

He smiled back, reciprocating the same.

"Any new powers I need to know about?" Uncle Mike asked in curiosity.

"No, Tio, the same," Alessandra said as Jonathan interrupted her.

"Well, I wanted to tell you about it, but we were about to engage in the bow-chika-wow-wow," he said in embarrassment.

"The what?" Uncle Mike asked in confusion.

"You don't want to know, Tio," Alessandra replied in embarrassment as Uncle Mike flashed a disgusted and annoyed look. Alessandra looked at Jonathan in curiousness and asked awkwardly, "What happened, Babe? *Did I flash in the act?* she wondered concerningly.

He looked at her with an edgy look and explained the scenario. "Well, it happened during our little bustle before you picked us up. She glowed in that yellow-orange glow in anger and then glowed an aqua-ish color in despair. She first did this when I told her she wasn't swinging from the chandelier," he confirmed.

Alessandra listened closely.

"She glowed dark neon green when crying, which I reassured her she there was no reason to spit from her eyes," he said in the sternness.

She looked at Uncle Mike and gave a warm smile and then immediately tried to recall what she felt.

"Do you remember what you were feeling, Mija?" Uncle Mike said, uncertain of what the cause of the glow was.

"No, Tio, I got a little distracted," she said shamefully.

"Carlos," he yelled and flashed a disappointed face from the rear-view mirror as they got closer to the studio door.

"Tio, I'm sorry," Jonathan said in fearful disappointment.

"I got a little sketched out as this has never happened, and I was losing focus on the space and time control in the molecular," Uncle Mike interrupted.

"I know what space and time control is. I don't need it followed with the technical term of it," Uncle Mike said. Uncle Mike faked a smile as he was approaching the barricaded blocks approaching the security guard.

"License and registration, sir," the police officer replied.

Alessandra was crotched up in curiosity as the voice was a familiar one from the past. "Officer Matthews," she said in surprise.

"Alessandra," he replied in surprise. "Oh my God, how have you been?" he said bewilderedly.

Jonathan rolled down the window and yelled, "Lieutenant Matthews," as the officer approached the back window.

He replied, "Major King," as he immediately gave a soldier salute.

"At ease, Lieutenant," he said in humbleness. "You know I am not into that greeting," he reassured.

"Sorry, sir, it's a habit," he opened the door as Jonathan got out of the car to embrace in a masculine hug and immediately got back into the vehicle.

"Wait, you know each other?" Alessandra asked in perplexity.

Jonathan looked at him smiled and said proudly, "He's my brother in arms in the Azulian Military Task Force.

Alessandra sat back in bewilderment as she tried to compose herself in perplexity.

"Is Officer Martinez ready for assault if anything goes astray?" he asked in the perfected-mimicking-tone Uncle Mike had.

Alessandra and Uncle Mike looked at each other from the rear-view mirror and nodded with an expression of approval.

"Let me introduce you to Generalissimo Miguel Rojelio Romero, our first Tourionian ranking officer," he introduced proudly.

The officer followed with a military salute and replied, "Officer Alejandro Matthews, sir, of the Azulian Military Task Force. It's an honor and a privilege and an honor to meet you face-to-face, sir," he said in a firm whisper as Uncle Mike reciprocated the salute.

"Officer Alejandro Martinez is ready for recon and secured and armed in the building, sir," he said in the same firm whisper.

"Thank you, soldier. At ease," Uncle Mike replied in humility.

"Wait, why is everyone name Alejandro?" Alessandra added. "Was my name Alessandra on purpose?" she asked curiously.

"You Babe, coincidence. Their name, not so much. I blame Lady Gaga for that one," he said jokingly.

Officer Matthews came back to his usual demeanor and said, “Fucken Gaga. But I love her. I’m glad she made it here in this world. She’s amazing,” he added in delight.

Alessandra thought for a minute and asked in eagerness, “So is Alejandro Martinez related to AR Jay?

“Your high school friend I met at the pageant at the Old Saint,” he said.

“No, Babe, he’s a normal person with a major purpose,” he said in reassurance.

“Do I find out that purpose?” she asked in anxiousness.

Uncle Mike replied in seriousness, looking at her in the rearview mirror. “If I tell you, I have to kill you. You’re royalty. You just need to worry about not getting killed. Got it,” he said earnestly.

“I will direct you to the drop-off point and escort you to your designated parking spot, Generalissimo Romero,” Officer Matthews demanded as he directed Uncle Mike to the drop-off location.

“If you need me, call out my name. And son,” He added anxiously.

“Yes, Tio,” Jonathan said before getting out of the vehicle.

Officer Matthews opened his door.

“Take care of our girl,” he said in a worrisome tone.

Jonathan smiled at Uncle Mike from the rear-view mirror. He replied reassuringly, “Precious Cargo,” as the screams got louder and lights brightened in the rhythmic flashing of patterns as Officer Matthews escorted Jonathan to Alessandra’s side and stayed looking at the ground in thought.

Uncle Mike asked as she finally gained control of the power as he replied uneasily, "What is it?"

Alessandra looked up and grinned as she realized he didn't read her thoughts and broke into seriousness as she said, "What is up with the fucken M last names?"

Alessandra blocked the flashing lights while she got out of the car. She tried to regain her consciousness as soon as she reached for Jonathan's hand. She stood up as she got out of the car and felt the breeze of the evening air hit her face as she looked back at the chiffon that fluttered in the wind. For a moment, she checked the surroundings as the sudden burst that flung her chiffon high low dress hit her lower calf. She could hear the excitement of so many familiar faces; her neighborhood yelling, "You did it, girl" and "Congratulations" for the news that just hit social media from a leaked source from the hotel they stayed.

Jonathan looked at her with pride and subtleness and stole another kiss. He stared at her and said with pride, "It's showtime Warrior Princess."

She looked at all the familiar faces. Some from college. Some for high school. Some from junior high as she gazed around in amazement. She shed a tear as she looked at Jonathan and said in exasperation, "I didn't know so many people cared."

"You're not just a Warrior Princess. You're beloved by everyone you touch," he reassured in humility. He added in amusement, saying, "I'm just the host and the stud walking the pride and joy of her barrio. Let's go save our people," he said adjectively.

Mathews approached the two and said, "Are we ready, team?"

Alessandra thought about the real reason they were there as she said, "Yes. It's on like *Donkey Kong*. Let's save mi gente," she added in stern affirmation.

Jonathan escorted her by the hand, and they both greeted them. Alessandra thought about the impeccable doom that was about to happen that night, which gave her more reason not to fail. She thought back about the first night she appreciated San Antonio. There were also many reasons Alessandra resented her hometown. She thought about her journal entry and the events that happened as she thought about the moments she had in Houston. The good. The bad. The ugly. She felt an overwhelming proudness and a new profound view of her new home. *I wouldn't have had everyone who I engaged in supporting me if I was in Houston*, she thought to herself.

No, you wouldn't, Babe. This is home. For you for us, Jonathan thought as he looked at Alessandra with a humble and proud smile.

Alessandra looked at him with a smile and thought, *You helped with that?*

Of course, I can hear you. Now that you have complete trust. Loud and clear, Jonathan looked at her lovingly as he reached in for a kiss.

She could hear two familiar voices telepathically.

One familiar male voice said, *I knew that bitch would make it*, which sounded like one of her childhood female friends.

The other saying, *That bitch looks fierce. I'm proud of you, sis,*" another said in admiration.

She yelled and said in curiosity as Matthews quickly begin to chase Alessandra in caution, surveying the surroundings. "AR, Jay? Christina?" Seeing their familiar faces, she screamed in delight, which followed with screams of pleasure from them.

"Yes, bitch, it's us," AR Jay and Christina yelled in delight as they jumped up and down in glee.

"Oh, my God!" Alessandra said as she hugged the two and cried. "I thought you guys were mad at me," she said as she wept.

"Do you think we would miss our girl's appearance as a Superstar?" as Christina mimicked Mary Catherine Gallegar from *Superstar*.

She wiped her tears as she laughed.

"Let's not mess up that fabulous makeup," AR Jay added in joy.

Jonathan came up and hugged the two as he said in delight, "It's good to see you guys."

"Hey, thanks for taking care of our girl man," AR Jay added, "congratulations, brother-in-law.

"Precious cargo and thank you, brother," as AR Jay and Jonathan shared a firm handshake.

"Babe, can we have them come backstage?" She expressed another hint, "As the craziness that's going to happen tonight?"

Jonathan nodded and called Matthews to bring their two friends now family over the red velvet rope.

Matthews blocked the crowd as Alessandra lifted the rope as they kneeled in to cross under the red velvet. Matthews looked at Alessandra and Jonathan and nodded to the question, asked telepathically by Alessandra, and the face that Jonathan knew what it signaled.

Matthews sighed and nodded in agreement as Alessandra replied, "I trust them, friends and family. If anyone has my back, it's them, no matter how crazy things get.

Jonathan looked at Alessandra in seriousness and said, "Let's get this party started."

AR Jay replied with, "Just like the old days."

Christina replied with, "I'll get the first round; it's going to be a wild night," as they began walking toward the door of the studio.

In a gentleman-like manner, Jonathan reached for Alessandra's hand as Matthews opened the door for the group, allowing the two friends to enter first as the two walked behind them.

Alessandra replied in a sarcastic monotone, saying to the two, "It's going to be apocalyptic."

Chapter 17

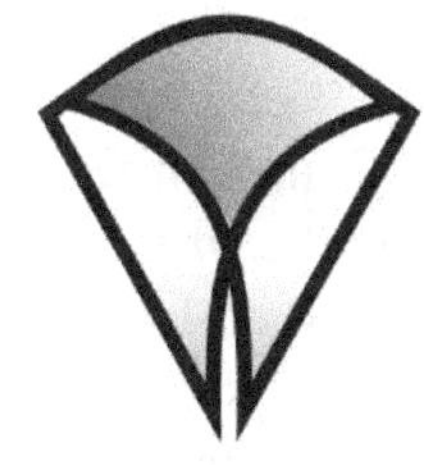

Alessandra looked from behind the stage to survey the audience. She saw that most of her neighborhood was seated in the front section. "I don't think that's the best place for my neighborhood to be sitting. The attacks probably focus on the filmed audience," which had Jonathan look at Alessandra and excused himself from the executives he was speaking with as AR Jay and Christina looked star-struck.

They saw some familiar famous people in the open dressing rooms where the celebrities were for hair and makeup. He looked at her in dismay and smiled quickly, not to give anyone who he was engaging in as he wasn't sure whether they were part of the legion.

Alessandra, being worried about her community's fate, couldn't help but not be able to tap into the thoughts of potential threats.

He could feel the worry and emotion now because of the connection they developed, which only meant her powers were potentially growing. He peeked out the curtain; screams from the audience erupted as he looked out and then popped his head back in. He turned to Alessandra, smiled and, leaned in for a kiss.

The executives escorted AR Jay and Christina to the opposite side of the stage.

In affirmation, Jonathan thought, *You're right. Let's usher them out of harm's way,* and walked to the producers. Jonathan asked to have some first rows of the audience moved as he used his arms to direct where he wanted. She saw Christina and AR Jay approaching her and peeped out as well to see what was happening.

AR Jay was wearing a swaggish brocade sports coat. Alessandra made the sports coat when she asked AR Jay to become one of the guest models for her graduation fashion design school. She mimicked the same pattern but in black and red, which buttoned midway, revealed a black button-up that complemented his toasty complexion accented with a red tie, with slacks and shiny shoes that reflected in the bright lights of the backstage. He was striking and charmingly handsome with hazel eyes and was averagely stocky, sporting a rhinestone stud on his right ear and wearing a faux hawk with dark brown hair.

Christina was wearing a strapless jumpsuit with a mauve collared detailing contrasted with the black material that had embossed dusty mauve pinstripes. She was averagely plump with brown eyes and an angelic face.

Christina wore her light brown hair half up with a messy bun and down with a subtle wave. She wore the rhinestone jewelry set encrusted with pale pink rhinestones. Claire's Boutique gifted them to her from when Christina made her first attempt for a fashion show during her Junior year at college. The jewelry complimented her fair complexion. She looked at the necklace and recalled that day.

"You still have that silly old thing?" she asked in amusement.

"Of course, girl. It's not a Tiffany ring, but it's priceless to me," she said in profound proudness.

She looked at AR Jay's brocade jacket in delight. "You still have that stupid old thing?"

He expressed his pride with an open-armed gesture as he said in delight, "Well, we had to rock your previous venture so we can market your talents other than being a tomcat."

"Bitch can I get into the adult industry so I can meet the love of my life too?" Christina teased.

"You guys are assholes," she scolded in playfulness.

"Well, you know you two set the standard for entertaining adult actors and the ability to step out of the adult film world," AR Jay replied in a cultivating manner.

"How so?" she asked alluringly.

"Well, *TMZ* reported today that the actors and actresses that are getting denied jobs with major film companies have hired a big-time law firm file a Discrimination Class Action Lawsuit. The suit maintains that they turned the actors down on roles they have exhibited exceptional thespian talent and gave it to someone mediocre in the role," he added.

"No, I didn't do that," she said as she shook her head doubtingly.

Christina nodded her head in admiration as she said, "You and Johnny are all over the media right now. Your picture at Hotel Emma is all over the internet about your engagement and how you and homeboy are the voice of the adult entertainment industry," she added.

"Our best friend and sister from another mister," he added as he nodded in praise and reached in for a hug.

Alessandra couldn't believe what she was hearing. It was like déjà vu all over again when she first found out about super biological abilities. She remained in the embrace as Christina came in to join in the unbreakable embrace. Alessandra cried again.

"I'm sorry for leaving as I did after our disagreement," she said in guilt.

"They pulled her away and looked at her, perplexed." AR Jay said in disbelief, "Why would we hold that against you, girl. You had a lot going on at the moment. You just worked yourself to death without taking time to deal with all the bullshit life threw at you. How dare you think we are that kind of people," AR Jay said in jokingly dismay.

Christina looked at AR Jay and then at Alessandra with a content smile as she said, "We are ride and die, girl. Forever."

Jonathan walked up behind them as he interrupted by saying, "Why wouldn't you think you could fuck shit up?" he said proudly.

"Thank you, bro," AR Jay said with a proud smile.

"Alessandra would rule the world!" Christina said proudly.

"Or if I have to save it," Alessandra said as she wiped the rest of her tears.

Jonathan looked at her with a surprised smirk.

"Yeah, Babe," he said as he added I need to talk to you telepathically.

"Well, guys, let me have a moment with my future husband, but let me have another moment with them?"

"Okay, Babe, we got to make sure we fix your eye makeup. You know I don't care how you look, but if anyone talks shit about your running makeup, I am going to fuck someone up," he said in a stern face that turned into a smirk.

"Don't worry about her face, brother-in-law," Christina said with a smile. "We always got her," she added.

"I hope so, guys," he said. "I'll see you in a few, Princess," as he snuck a kiss and stepped out to the stage.

"Hey Al," AR Jay said in suspicion.

"What's up, AR Jay?" she asked with a suspicious face.

"Don't get offended when I say this, but how does he know to come? It's like he's psychic," he said in suspicion. "Can he read my mind?" he asked.

"Leave them alone, broseph," Christina added in defense.

They heard Jonathan talk about the events that happened and the announcement of their engagement, which made the whole auditorium scream saying "Viva San Antonio" and "Way to rep SA girl" as the crowd cheered in delight.

They looked at the stage and gave that oh shit surprised look.

"No, really, girl, is he psychic?"

Alessandra flashed a silly smile and said, "No guys. I'm marrying a badass. He's my badass and my person," she said lovingly. "Now, let's get you beautified," she added. They walked to the open dressing area where hair and makeup were at; she jokingly said, "I don't need to rep San Antonio looking like a fucken hot mess."

They looked at each other, remembering saying what they said when they got ready for prom in high school and recited in blissful unison, "Touché motherfuckers. Touché."

"Five minutes, Babe," Jonathan said telepathically.

"Can we stop moving before I am forced to go looking like this?" Alessandra insisted.

AR Jay replied in confidence as he said, "Bitch, have we ever let you down?"

She stared at Christina for a second and then at AR Jay as she said in comfort, "Never."

Christina clapped her hand in earnestness as she said, "Let's get her done."

Chapter 18

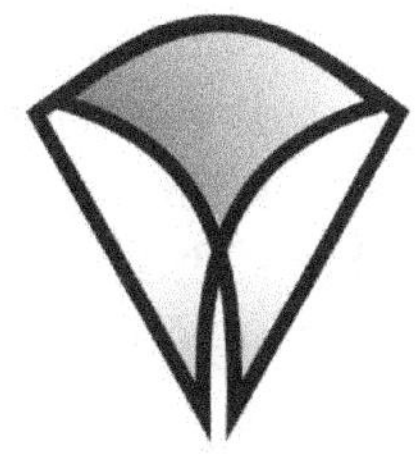

It was about to be intermission as Alessandra paced back and forth near the dressing tables that her friends were lounging around.

"How did Jasmine get a spot with her no-talent ass?" Christina said out loud in disappointment. She looked up as she saw her friend pacing back and forward.

"She's probably sleeping with one producer," AR Jay said in the same tone.

"She's probably sleeping with one of the producer's Babe," Jonathan said in an amusing tone telepathically.

Alessandra broke out in laughter.

"I thought I would make you laugh since you're feeling many ways right now," Jonathan said refreshingly.

"Thanks, Babe," she responded in reassurance.

AR Jay looked at Alessandra with the same resting bitch face that she flashed years ago, saying in joy, "It's about time you laugh, girl."

Christina laughed and responded in seriousness as she replied, “I bet Jonathan is thinking the same thing we all are thinking about Jasmine,” rolling her eyes, saying her name.

“I bet you he is,” Alessandra reassured.

“So, what is going on in your mind right now, girl?” AR Jay said with a stern smile.

“You’re not getting cold feet, are you?” Christina said concerningly.

“No, girl. I love that man. Besides, after all, I put him through, he earned shackling me to a ball and chain now,” she said with a humble sigh.

AR Jay and Christina looked at one another with a too familiar grin. Alessandra tried to hold her laugh as she knew what they were going to say. She was concerned about looking like a freak of nature in front of them but couldn’t stop laughing.

Christina replied, looking at AR Jay in humor, saying, “You were thinking it.”

They both replied in chorus, bursting out in laughter, both pointing to Alessandra as they said, “You said it.”

Alessandra followed with “Ha” in Wayne’s Brother's impression as Jonathan delivered reassurance.

“They would never think that about you. Your friends never have. They may freak out, but they will think you’re a badass. Like me,” he consoled.

“Thanks, Babe,” she replied as AR Jay looked worried.

“Is it like that time we had in high school where you thought something awful was going to happen and didn’t catch our friend from committing suicide in the locker-room?” he said sadly mournfully.

"Yes, but it's different," she added.

"Don't tell me it's a repeat of nine eleven," Christina said in fearful dismay.

Alessandra looked at them and said, "I hope not," as she said hopefully.

"Girl, tell us what it is," AR Jay said consolingly.

"You know you can trust us," Christina said trustingly.

They all had that grieving face as they sat in silence, thinking about the tragic event in worry.

AR Jay broke the silence as he said proudly, "Well, if they fuck with us, they will see how the Westside fights, shanks and all," he said in comfort, looking at his sisters in reassurance. They heard Jasmine's flirtatious attempts as they laughed, hearing Jonathan's rebuttal.

"This bitch," Jonathan delivered annoyingly.

The three heard Jonathan's polite annoyance as his voice echoed from backstage. "You're not my cup of tea. Besides, I am marrying my person," as the crowd laughed.

Alessandra felt the unsettling feeling Jonathan developed.

They saw Jasmine exiting stage right by one producer of the show. Jasmine looked at the three and gave a dismissed look, followed by an embarrassing chuckle as the five-foot British man dressed like the passenger escorted Jasmine off the stage. It followed with an alarming feeling that she felt as Jonathan develops. The duo saw the unsettling look their dear friend developed, followed by the same look.

AR Jay replied with uneasiness, "Do I get the shanks ready?"

"Christina replied as she followed Alessandra's same look and said, "Ride or die mother fuckers, ride, or die."

Jonathan came in with a coy smile trying to break the ice, "Hey guys enjoying the show?"

The two gave a dismissive stare and began plotting, which Alessandra thought in amazement, *I got some badass friends*.

Jonathan grabbed Alessandra gently by the arm and said, "Excuse me guys, I'm going to steal my bride away so we can," which he paused, giving them the eyebrow expression.

They smiled dismissively and began thinking about how they would get their beloved city out of danger.

Jonathan escorted Alessandra into the dressing room on the far-right side of the corridor behind the backstage. He shut the door gently as he looked at Alessandra in alarm. "That's one of his goons. Did he look at you? Did he notice you?" Jonathan said in concern.

"No, Babe, Jasmine gave the stink face and followed that creepy guy toward the back but didn't even bother to look at me," she said.

"I think she's going to be the science project in the zombifying to see if they have the ability here," he said, concerned. "I noticed that his thumb was turning into a talon as I zoomed in to inspect closer."

The auditorium music got louder. A few seconds after, they heard a scream. They both immediately bolted out of the room to find AR Jay and Christina underneath the dressing room tables in fright.

She looked at her friends as Jonathan stood back in concentration as he gained control of the surrounding space. Alessandra stared at their friends with a concerned face that had her radiate a faint glow.

"What the fuck, Alessandra?" What are you not telling us? They said in fear.

"I'll explain later," she said in alarm. "Get everyone out of here before it gets worse," she said in a hurry as she ran toward the screams.

Jonathan followed and paused for a moment, helping her friends from underneath the table; they reached in hesitation and smiled in comfort as he said, "She's special. Ensure everyone gets out safe and fast." He ran in Alessandra's direction as they stood up, which the two instantly followed to make sure their girl was okay.

When they reached the second filming stage, they saw Jonathan glowing in an aqua neon light as he saw the wound that dripped in blood heal. They heard a groan as they saw Alessandra deliver a running kick, which was seven feet off the ground that ended up deflecting a shadowing light in a golden-white glow to deflect the seven-foot crouched creature as she yelled, "Tio."

She screamed as she glanced at Jonathan as he finished healing Jasmine. Alessandra screamed in excitement, "I fucken got my powers down."

Jasmine opened her eyes; as she regained consciousness, she stared in shock, which resulted in an immediate fearful scream that sounded like the cliché girl in scary movies.

Jonathan looked up at the two as they also screamed as they followed with "Holy fuck!"

Jonathan interrupted and said, "Can we get this basic bitch to safety?"

They came to her aid.

Jonathan demanded in his Uncle Mike tone, “Run as fast as you can out and exit the center front stage stairs into the auditorium.”

They shook their head in fearful shock.

Jonathan ordered, “Hey, snap out of it and hurry. I got recon waiting.”

They nodded in brave fear and helped Jasmine.

They heard Alessandra groan in pain followed by an aqua glow as they saw her jump in a stance as she dodged the Beast’s talon attack.

Jonathan looked at them and followed with the same tone, “Hey, she’s a mother fucken Star Girl” as he ran toward the Beast. He sped up like a lightning bolt with a vertical flying punch as he went to help.

The three looked for a split second in shock as they said, “Alessandra is a fucken superhero.”

Chapter 19

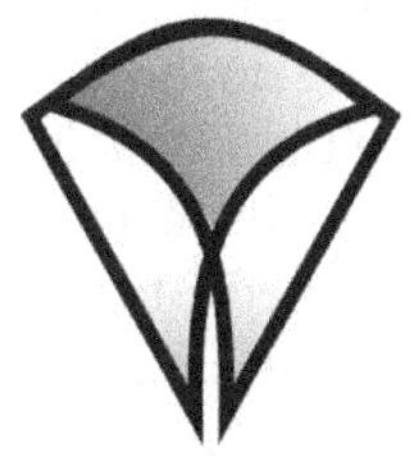

The Beast was a brownish-green furry creature that flashed red eyes. Its talons, red eyes, and had fangs that looked like big shark teeth. Its mouth hung low, protruding clear white ooze that dripped from its mouth like clear caramel. The bald creature's patches stood tall.

Jasmine, finally gained strength, broke away, and asked others, “What the hell was that?”

Matthew met them in the middle of the stage to help any wounded who might have been remaining.

Matthew yelled, “Hurry,” as he glowed a light blue glow.

Martinez directed the trio as they looked back as he was leading the traffic out the door. Martinez looked around and nodded to Matthews as he hurried out the door.

“Anyone injured?” he asked in a scuffle.

AR Jay responded in a slight panic, catching his breath as he gained composure. “Only Jasmine, but Jonathan did this glowing thing that healed her.

He looked at Jasmine and immediately asked in confirmation, “How do you feel?”

Jasmine replied, still in a panic, trying to sort the events, “What the fuck was that?” Jasmine was wearing a strapless glittered and rhinestone dress, which resembled a pageant dress that drug on the floor with a flowing train, stained with patches of blood that looked like giraffe spots.

He gave her an annoyed look and said, “I can see she’s fine.” He turned to Christina and asked concerningly, “How are Alessandra and Jonathan?”

Christina smiled in shocking amazement and said, “Our girl’s the real-life Wonder Woman.”

Matthews replied in a corrective manner, saying, “She’s not Wonder Woman. She’s actually from a linage Amazonian, Aztec, Mayan, and Incan decent.”

She looked in disappointment and then recognized him in surprise and replied, “Matthews? The same Matthews during her pre-shot mess days?”

He dismissed Christina as he said in profound sincerity, “We can catch up on this reunion later. Let’s get you all to safety.”

They bolted to exit, and ran out through the double doors of the studios. They could see the crowd clearing from the front of the street, heading toward McCullough. The farthest of the guests were running past San Antonio College and somehow heading toward San Pedro Park.

The trio looked back at the studio's five-story building and immediately whipped around, hearing a peel out echoing in the studio's parking garage. They immediately turned to Matthews, which eased their nerves as he calmly was on his cellphone, having a direct and tactful conversation with someone. They saw the silver rouge glistening in the night that pulled up to the street sidewalk. As the tinted window rolled down, they immediately expressed a wide-opened mouth shocked facial expression.

Uncle Mike grinned from the window as he said coyly, “Look, time to see the troublemakers.” He flashed a cheeky to joyous cheek grin as he looked glanced for a few seconds to AR Jay and then to Christina seeing the same reaction. He looked at Jasmine as she looked at the duo of friends, and then Uncle Mike consecutively as he signaled the team for confirmation. “Who’s the basic bitch?”

Jasmine was looking at Uncle Mike in annoying disappointment.

Christina looked at Uncle Mike in amazement as he said, “Let’s cut the reunion and get you three out of harm’s way.”

AR Jay stomped his foot, finally breaking his shocked looked and said protesting, “With all due respect, sir, I am not leaving our girl like we did when she faced danger back then. We weren’t there to help her fight; we are here now, dammit,” he replied in pride.

Christina looked at AR Jay and then Uncle Mike with the same protest saying, “Ride and die bitches. Ride and die.”

Jasmine looked at them in disappointment and then followed the same protest. “Fuck this, I’m going to,” she demanded, looking at the two in shocked dismay.

AR Jay looked at her as her look changed, looking surprised, saying, "Jasmine, you always hated Alessandra," he insisted.

She looked at him and said annoying, "No, I never hated her. I just hated that she was a better person than me."

"Since you all want to go on a suicide mission, let's arm you with some things to at least try not to get killed and get our girl her suit. She's going to need it with you dumbasses."

They heard the peel out of brakes pulling up, Matthews looked toward Martinez and looked at Uncle Mike, saying, "No need Generalissimo. We got you covered."

Uncle Mike looked at AR Jay and Christina in a jokingly disappointing look saying, "Why couldn't all you dumb asses be as proactive as Matthews?"

Matthews pulled out Alessandra's suit from the car. The suit floated like it was on an invisible hanger. He nodded in satisfaction.

Christina said in a wowed, loud expression, "Damn. She puts superheroes to shame now."

Shattered glass and stee materialized into dust power as they saw Jonathan and Alessandra running out of the building in panic.

"Get in the car." Christina added, "AR Jay, get in the car. I need my co-pilot," as they got closer to the door. She looked surprised as she saw Jasmine run into the car as they reached the threshold of the door.

"What is she doing?" she yelled as they arranged themselves, seeing Jasmine try to fit in the back seat. She slapped her hand on her forehead as they went down the first flight of concrete stairs, saying, “Jasmine goes in the hatchback trunk.”

Jasmine jumped to the back, stumbling into the trunk of the hatchback.

“You need to change to your suit,” Uncle Mike yelled.

“Yeah, I'm so fucken sure I have time, Tio!”

They approached the middle of the second to the last flight of stairs.

“What was the proudest moment of your life? Make the gesture you did then,” he insisted.

Christina and AR Jay looked at each other in confirming smile and yelled, “Junior high fashion show. Superstar the motherfucker.”

She shrugged in embarrassment and quickly stole a kiss from Jonathan. “Don’t judge me.”

He ran to the car Matthews and Martinez were in and were reaching the last flight of stairs as the creature was visibly running toward the door.

The three friends looked in shock as they said, “Holy Fuck!”

They saw Alessandra jumping in a ray of multiple colors of bright light. She began as a bright purple color.

Seeing the garment bag, Matthews was carrying go from puffy to flat as they turned a confusing set of glances, looking toward the opposite car. They stared at the radio reading *Blinding Lights* by The Weeknd, then looking at the phones now playing the intro to the song, followed by the revving of the engine from the car in front of it as Alessandra gracefully and quickly landed in front of the driver side door. She turned to everyone in the car and said, “I forgot to tell you. I’m a superhero.”

They stared in shock, the suit began flashing multiple color lights from the armor. They looked at the panting monstrous creature and yelled in panic as he was now on the last flight of stairs.

"You know I am proud of you, baby girl, but it's time to book it." Jonathan buckled up his seatbelt. "Hey guys buckle up," and looked back at Jasmine, saying, "You, hold on tight." Jonathan jumped into the middle from the moon roof that Uncle Mike left open from the hotel. Rushing into the middle of Uncle Mike and Christina, he quickly adjusting himself, looking at Alessandra with a proud smile. "Show them what you got, Princess," he said without hesitation.

"You got it, Charming," she said as she punched up, raveling the purpose of the suit as she smiled and screamed "Fuck Yeeesssss!" as she threw out a blast of flashing yellow and orange rays. The rays pierced through the Beast's shoulder, followed by a painful growl that ended and knocked the creature down. The crowd yelled in praise, which stopped immediately after the creature got up.

"Now it's time, bolt!" She revved up the engine, which followed the opposite car to take off, which followed her after seeing the creature dividing into a second smaller beast that looked like a mutated cougar hyena that chased them.

She looked at the guys as she said, "Vamanos!" She looked at Jasmine, speaking in a monotone, "Hi Jasmine," following the song paused five seconds to restart from the beginning. She made the first turn as she drifted and ended up passing the first light that turned into McCullough thinking, *I hope they can hear me?*

"Loud and clear, Princess Alessandra," the two confirmed as the suit vibrated on her right shoulder.

She saw that she passed Lulu's Café and turned to Jonathan and then her uncle as Jonathan said, "You can communicate with anyone who's on the assigned mission," he said proudly.

She smiled and passed the light following the car in front of her as she saw both creatures now getting closer. They began approaching as the creatures got on the entrance ramp of 281, growling in anger, running faster, and getting closer.

"I see them approaching Your Highness; what to do, Generalissimo Romero?" Matthews asked as Alessandra saw him popping out to get a glimpse of what they were dealing with.

"Wait, Your Royalty?" Jasmine said in shock.

She looked back at Jasmine with a grin and a proud smile to AR Jay and Christina as she said humbly, "I am also a Princess" and looked at AR Jay saying, "Fast and Furious time." She climbed out the moon roof as he quickly took the seat and the wheel.

"Come get a piece of Alpo shit," Alessandra said as the two heard a quick jump that had secured her on the roof of the car.

Jonathan looked at AR Jay and said, "Don't worry, she won't fall, drive fast."

He blasted out of the car like a firework on the Fourth of July, which resulted in fireballs passing the side of the vehicle.

They all screamed as AR Jay said, "Holy shit, I'm going to die."

Chapter 20

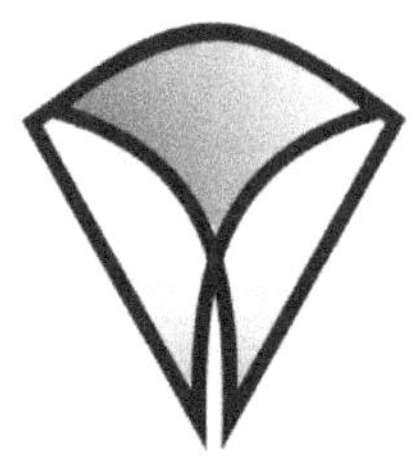

Alessandra looked behind her as the first beast fell to the ground and died. She noticed that the car was far behind the damage and quickly charged toward the vehicle in mid-flight as Jonathan deflected the attack with his might.

He saw the other vehicle coming back to the opposite side of the freeway. As it exited, cars were on both sides of the median with pedestrians running to safety. The beast ended, falling to its right side.

"You have impeccable timing to Babe," he said as he got up.

"Who thought I would be your knight and shining armor," she replied.

The suit that she wore was a light rose romper in the same material that was a lighter version of the armory's insulation, embossed with breastplates, shoulder plates, and a hip plate that looked titanium in rose gold metallic shine. She had a warrior skirt that was high, low, and was a deep rose. She looked back and saw the car was out of sight, which followed her signature fighting stance. The beast got up as he appeared to grow stronger. She jumped and pulled out her Sai strapped to her thigh, now exposed as she pierced, pulling her Lara Croft move that just agitated the beast.

"Why isn't this fucker dying?" she asked as it was the steroid version of the one she killed.

"This cock sucker has an internal armor that is materialized by the attacks the other took," he said. He attempted to strike with the air kick Uncle Mike did in the armory, which put the beast on his back deployed as Jonathan yelled to Alessandra, "Ticking timebomb."

She looked at Jonathan and smiled, which she tried to repel but wasn't working. Matthews and Martinez were in the obstacle course of vehicles from the pile-up from the fight. "It's not working, Babe," she yelled in concern.

The beast got up and began attacking as Jonathan yelled, "Think of something."

Alessandra looked lost as she figured out what she could use to evoke the power. The beast pinned Jonathan down as it erected a tongue that looked like something from *Aliens*.

Jonathan was losing strength until he snapped as he said, "Derrick!"

Alessandra quickly filled with rage as she glowed. Still, this time an electric, intense dark pink as Jonathan said, "Holy Shit!"

A powerful blast from Alessandra finally broke Jonathan free to control the surrounding space. Matthews and Martinez stopped in their tracks as a worrying fear appeared on their face. The stress made Alessandra more dangerous as she turned a mauve color as she appeared angrier.

Jonathan looked at her controlling the surrounding area, and said, “Babe, don’t lose control.” He saw her as she turned a neon magenta. “No Babe, don’t do it; you’re my person.”

She appeared dark and evil, his voice softened her back, slowly returning to her original hot pink color.

Jonathan said, “Tio Mike,” which ended up condensing the beast with a blast as it exploded.

She condensed into the ball of energy and materialized just as the creature turned into dust.

She looked in pride and then in fear as she looked perplexed, and said, “What is happening?” She saw Jonathan approach her.

He gently secured her shoulders as she looked down. He said, “It's human nature. We can go either way depending on the person, but you’ll never be evil as long as I am around.” He stole a kiss.

They embraced in the *Notebook* kiss as they heard “Your Highness, Lieutenant lookout!”

An ancient spear hurled their way that Jonathan deflected.

“No!” Alessandra cried, looking at where the spear was coming. She saw Antonio Castillo suspended in the air as she fell with Jonathan gently on the floor. Matthews and Martinez kneeled beside them. He saw the man who had Abuela trapped in his arms, covering her mouth, turn into the crowned fog figure in her dream.

“We finally meet Alessandra, Princess of the Itzicanina creed,” he said in a haunting voice.

"If I can't take San Antonio, it will give me great pleasure to take your protector Mara Santiago Romero," he said as he disappeared into thin air.

She looked at Jonathan in fear as she said in a panic, "Baby, Charming, are you okay?" holding back tears.

He smiled as he jokingly said in painful groans, "It's only a scratch. I'll be fine."

"Lieutenant, you want us to recon the threat?"

He looked at them, shaking his head in a gentle no, and looked at Alessandra as he said, "She's ready."

Alessandra couldn't stop looking at her, having tears fall from her eyes. He reached with a weak hand as he wiped her tears and said, "It's not your fault. Now go save Abuela."

"I don't even know where she is," she said in sad dismay.

"Close your eyes," he said as he coughed up blood. "Feel Abuela's fear and go from there."

The surrounding disaster disappeared, and the cool air turned into arid and intense heat, hearing the crackling of molten rock and echoes in a tavern. She opened her eyes and found herself in the same scenario from the first dream where she was on top of the boulder but with lakes of moving magna which looked like mushroom tops from the *Alice and Wonderland* cartoon she used to watch with Abuela when she got scared.

"Mi Nina," she heard in the echoes, followed by distinct sounds of male and female groans and painful screams. Abuela is a cage suspended by her arms and legs. She secured herself in the middle of a platform, and Alessandra could see looking at her demonic faces that resembled the faces of the campers in her dream when they secured her down. She looked at the floor as she panicked, seeing the faces of tortured dead looking at her erringly and demonically saying, “Come to us. Come here, little girl.”

Alessandra said in fearful hesitation, “Abuela, I’m coming.” She tried to find her way through the molten maze of various heights of jagged plateaus as she reached the halfway point to Abuela. It was here where she heard a demonic laugh. As she turned to subtle instinctiveness, she saw the mutilated body of a once Antonio Castillo who looked at her with evil indulgence.

“Your soul is mine, you broke ugly bitch,” he said in a demonic and confident way. She looked at the figure that reconstructed itself. It tore itself apart to reveal a half-naked man wearing an Aztec belt with a ravaged chest exposing the muscle and bone of an once Antonio Castillo. He was holding a loin cloth fastened by an Aztec inscribed belt bearing his muscular buttocks. His mutilated face was like the foggy face she saw in her dream, which exposed the real face of the Mictlantecuhtli and revealed a part of the brain that pulsated in a tortoise-like pace.

She took another look at him up and down at a glacial pace as she replied in sarcasm, “Have you seen yourself in the mirror? You sorry excuse of a pageant reject.”

“You’re a foolish broke bitch aren’t you,” he shrieked in rage.

“Not only are you a sorry excuse of a pageant reject, but you don’t even know proper hygiene.” Alessandra made a disgusted face as she fanned the air and majestically positioned in her fighting stance. “I’m going to have to clean that mouth out and have you call me mama,” she replied as she blocked the first attack.

"I can't wait to bend you over and hear you scream for Papa to stop," he said in demonic pleasure, which followed a deflection from the bolt of green energy she released as he flung it to the neighboring boulder.

"The only saying is your daddy now is you after I bend you over motherfucker," she said as he pierced her Sai through the shoulder.

He spoke tongue as the tavern shook, splashing the thick magma into the air. Mictlantecuhtli materialized into black smoke, which started the quakes to become more violent as he erected slowly from the twenty-foot tavern's grounds. She saw the face of the now demonic zombie looking campers swaying like a cobra in the air protruding from the small of his back. They struck her as she deflected with a ground roll, losing emotion from her power. The male head of the camper led a second attack.

Alessandra jumped up and blasted him with a burst of yellow-orange rays that decapitated the male head. The head fell into the magma as the head growled in agony. The smell of burned hair and flesh filled the dry, dense air.

As she landed, she took out the Sai piercing the neck that had her slide with the blade horizontally as the other head growled in pain, as the head fell apart, falling into the lava. Flames blasted Alessandra from the mouth of the skull that blasted her down to the tavern floor as she burned. The armor glowed in lavender, which only healed to tolerable pain.

Mictlantecuhtli slowly shrank to normal size as he laughed demonically. He picked up Alessandra by the neck and choked her. She broke free as he crushed the other side of the skull, exposing the other part of his brain. He took the Kitana out of her holster with lighting speed that bared the Abuela's family crest as she stabbed him in the shoulder that protruded black ooze as he shrank to the size of Alessandra.

She screamed in agony as Abuela cried in pain but encouraging infliction, "You can do this." He flashed out an ancient Aztec knife and stabbed her in the other shoulder, which made her scream in more agonizing screams as Abuela gasped in fear, trying to fight off the demonic faces turned to her, trying to bite her.

"Use your healing power," she said.

She thought of the night that she glowed an aqua-ish lavender." She remembered Jonathan, which worked and gave her the strength to stand up. Recalling how she left Jonathan evoked her rage, which immediately turned her into neon hot pink as she blasted the ball of energy, remembering what Jonathan taught her before his injury, which made him flinch but still approached her. She got angrier, having her turn to a dark magenta, which made him flinch a few inches back. He continued to approach her, which had her rage growing and turned her into a neon blood red. Her entire body flame was like the phoenix tales her Uncle Mike used to tell her about the firebird's legend that flew in the South American Rain Forest; his Abuelo used to say to him as a kid.

Abuela yelled in fearful concern, "Resist his power. Resist his evil pull." Seeing that he was reaching for his shoulder just like Jonathan would and morphing into Jonathan began the evil manipulation.

Alessandra immediately stopped glowing as she found herself in the hotel room.

"High, Babe," Jonathan said.

"I had a horrible dream," she said in confusion as she had a weird dream that she was asleep.

Jonathan smiled his charismatic grin and replied consolingly, "Let's leave this all behind, Babe. Let's go far away from this world and this reality." And as he stole a peck, he got up and opened the draws to pack the items they left behind.

"Wait, Babe, what's wrong? You're acting differently. Why do you want to leave this? Leave destiny," she asked in confusion as she followed him in confusion, now wearing her original dress as the high low train fluttered in creepy silence.

He turned and yelled at her for the first time as he replied in anger, "Are you fucken stupid Babe? Do you want to get killed? Do you want to see me die again?" he demanded.

"You're right, Babe," she said in embarrassment.

"You see what happens when you get powers? You think and get arrogant and cocky," he said in disappointment.

She looked at the shirts lying on the bed, glancing at the shirt that said, "I'm marrying a badass. He's my badass." They stared intensely at the one that said, "I'm marrying a badass. She's my badass and my person," as the suspicions she was having made perfect sense. She looked at Jonathan and said, "You're my person, Charming."

He replied with, "Yeah, Babe, my person too."

Alessandra walked up to him and pecked him on the lips as he wrapped his arms around her. She said, "Can we stop by the store you got these shirts from? I want to see if they have matching cups," she said humorously.

"Yeah, sure, Babe," he dismissed her as he went back to packing. He felt a sharp stabbing pain as he looked out and yelled, "Noooooo!" as they found themselves both back in the tavern, now shaking more violently as the tavern shook, having pieces of rock splashing into the ground.

Alessandra ran to the now materialized cage of corpses as Abuela yelled in minor pain, cursing in Spanish. She smiled and ran to Abuela as she helped her up, saying, "Hola Abuela."

Abuela looked at her as she said proudly, "I knew you were always pure of heart."

Alessandra looked at Mictlantecuhtli as he morphed into what looked like the beast in her dream, saying, "Let's get out of this pinche chingadera" as they jumped the boulders as the tavern slowly caved in with the blast of the fire extinguishing out the beast's mouth. They reached the end of the tavern as the fire got closer. She jumped and zipped thru the air as she knocked the beast to the ground using and diving with her Katana in hand, aiming for the creature to disable the creature's quickness but didn't. She flew back to where Abuela was standing and looked at her, doing the same eyebrow expression Jonathan did. When she looked at Abuela, she saw a moment of grief and said, "It's your life before mine. Now climb!"

The beast flew toward Abuela as she scaled the cavern. She continued to attack the creature but was too late as it gained back its strength. Abuela was on the tavern's first plateau when the Beast roared and knocked her off, having Abuela hold on for dear life.

Alessandra punched the creature as she shot up with a neon green bolt of light. Next, Alessandra followed with a powerful punch with hot pink force as she erected her way to a now falling Abuela. She caught Abuela before reaching the magma that was now surrounding the entrance. She flew up to the top of the cavern, looking at Abuela with pride and said, "I guess I have more powers now."

She placed Abuela on the tavern's top exit and told Abuela, "Take care of Jonathan if I don't make it," as she jumped down with graceful and robust force.

The creature looked at her, roaring in a demonically demonic tongue that translated into English, "Once a broke bitch, you're dying a broke cheap bitch," as Abuela echoed in the cavern.

"Si Se Puede," which had Alessandra remembering a song Abuela sang to her while she scratched her, rocking her to sleep.

Alessandra yelled, "Si Se Puede. Con el alma de mi gente. Por Que soy Fuerte y Bella. Nace en la Sangre de las Mujeres podcrosas de las Mujeres de la Itzicanina."

The cavern shook and evoked lighting inside. The creature and Alessandra saw a sword and shield fall from a black hole lighting ridden portal, landing right in front of Alessandra.

She saw the creature vibrate. "You fucken cheap bitch," as it cocked its head back to release its last attack.

Alessandra thought of Jonathan as the creature moved in slow motion. She grinned in pride as she pulled the sword out of the ground blasting toward the Beast. "This cheap, broke bitch is now a priceless broke bitch motherfucker." Alessandra stabbed the neck of the beast.

The creature resumed its original speed, releasing the flame prematurely as she deflected in the air. The shield absorbed the flames. The shield glowed as it deflected the flame.

"Ala chingada!" Abuela blurted in astonishment.

The beast glowed, flashing the colors. Alessandra released a spectrum of lights as the beast yelled in mourning and painful agony. The creature mummified and burst into dust as she landed in a pacing and graceful way, looking at Abuela with a grin cheek to cheek as she blasted her way to Abuela.

"Mira la girl," she said jokingly, mocking her granddaughter's peers, saying, "She's a bad bitch this Vata loca."

"Okay, Abuela," she looked in, confused.

Alessandra heard Jonathan. "Come to me, my bride, my Princess, my person," and found herself back in the armory where her friends, her Uncle Mike, Martinez, and Matthews were and saw Jonathan weaker than before fighting for life. He smiled proudly in a weakened state as he said in a weak whisper, "Yay," and coughed. "You got your full powers."

Chapter 21

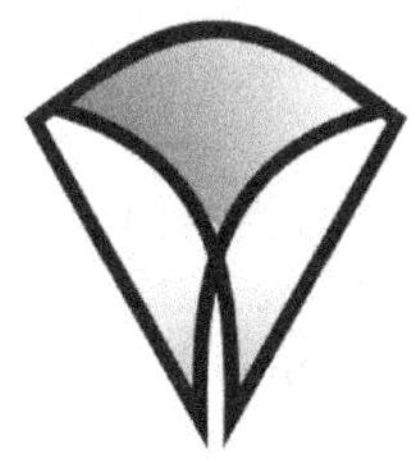

Alessandra ran to Jonathan as all her memories started rushing through her head. Their first encounter, their fight, their reunion in Houston, followed by her first night after she left a week after thinking about the night Christina and AR Jay came by after their breakup, bringing takeout from the Chinese Kitchen in Room 304 at the Red Roof Inn on Rittman Road. along with a bunch of chick flicks she loved to watch and enjoyed so much. The one that ended up making her mourn the loss of her Uncle Mike for the first time and then following her breakup's mourning. The phones started the theme song from the movie Aerosmith's *I Don't Want to Miss a Thing a Thing.* Alessandra broke up in a mournful cry as she ended up falling to her knees as she grabbed Jonathan's weak reach for her hand.

"I told you, you could do it, Babe." He looked at her with a soft and proudly adoring tone of amazement.

The entire room teared up as Abuela held back tears as she approached the two looking at Jonathan, brushing his face. Jonathan looked up at Abuela, saying in weak pride, "I told you she was always going to be pure of heart," as he coughed in gurgling agony as he looked back at Alessandra, and he smiled through his tears. "Star-crossed lovers, I guess," he said coaxingly.

"Don't leave me, Jonathan. I can't do this without you," she pleaded.

"You already did, Babe. I told you I was marrying a badass," he whispered. He lifted his other hand, pressing the ring he gave to her on her left finger, looking back at her and giving a weaker smile, saying, "You're still wearing it."

"Oh, course I'm wearing it. I am always going to wear it. Till the end."

"I'll always love you to the end and beyond," he said in a weakening tone.

"Jonathan, don't leave me," she pleaded. "Don't leave me, Charming," she pleaded again as she broke down.

He wearingly brushed her hair out of her face. "I'll never leave you. You'll always be my person no matter where I go," he promised.

"How can I do this without you? You keep me from being a ticking timebomb."

"Think of me, Mi Princessa. I'll always guide you through the darkest of nights like I always have. Nothing will change," he said in a weakened, comforting tone as tears fell from his eyes.

"I'm sorry I didn't marry you sooner." She laid her head on his for one last time.

He looked at her as he looked deep in her torn eyes as she looked at Jonathan smiling in mourning as Jonathan revealed one last gift while she looked in surprise as he whispered, "You'll always take my breath away," as he made the song played. He stole one last *Notebook* kiss that Alessandra indulged one last time.

His lips stopped moving.

"Jonathan," Alessandra yelled. Jonathan."

Uncle Mike walked to Alessandra and kneeled next to her with tears and said, "Alessandra, he's gone."

The room grew silent as they watched Alessandra sank into her Uncle Mike as she yelled, echoing in the tavern like a heartbroken ghost in the night.

"Nooooo," she yelled as she cried in a mighty waterfall of mournful tears.

The music continued to play as Alessandra cried in the starry cave that continued to glow like Jonathan's essence that danced along the cave walls among the celestial shine of the tavern roof through the mournful cries of the August night. Her family, including a new member, remained silent, crying the tears that Alessandra mourned for the love that was forever eternal, forever pure, eternally grateful, and pure of many moments of happy bliss. They all stood in mourning for their superhuman friend. They felt her heart shatter like never before as she saw the love of her entire life die right in front of her. They were proud of their friend, the Warrior Princess, who, no matter the sacrifices, selflessly saved the fate of their friends and the entire city.

Two days later was the funeral that touched the heart of the entire community. Alessandra mourned through the entire event. The hardest part of the service was seeing Abuela holding her granddaughter tight, saying, "I wish your Tio were here," having her father join in saying, "I know Mija. He was like a son too" as they followed in grief that was not as strong as hers.

Simultaneously, "TAPS" played while they handed her the folded-up flag during the traditional five-gun salute. Abuela and her father were heartbroken as they lowered him. Alessandra said in excruciating mourning, "Don't leave me Charming," which had AR Jay, Christina, and Jasmine crying in painful tears as they attempted to confront their friend.

Alessandra's friends asked if she wanted to gather with the family at the house.

"I'm going to the hotel that Jonathan Carlos and I were at," which followed with more tears as she replied, "since it was our pre-honeymoon excursion."

Jasmine was the first to reach in for a hug as the rest joined in with tears and sucking it in to gain composure for the sake of their friend.

Alessandra pulled back as she insisted, "I just need some time for myself."

Christina replied in concern, "I know you have a bottle of Jack in the room. Feel what you feel and start healing," she said apathetically

AR Jay touched Alessandra's cheek and said, "Jonathan wouldn't want to see you like this. And Uncle Mike would Drill Sergeant your ass if he did."

She flashed a fake smile and said, "I know," as she turned to Matthews and Martinez, they saluted her as she broke down and reached in for a hug that they both embraced. She wiped her tears as she composed herself, swallowed down the tears and said, “Take me to the hotel”, which followed with a tearful whimper, “please.”

“Yes, your Highness.”

She locked arm to arm with her two warriors as she excused themselves from the group.

AR Jay yelled out and said demandingly, “Hey guys.”

The two warriors looked back.

“Take care of our girl.”

Christina and Jasmine stood, demanding approval.

Matthews broke gently from Alessandra and turned around to give them an approving salute as he said, “Sir, yes sir.”

They provided an informal salute as he turned back around to put his left hand on the middle of her back as they escorted Alessandra to the black vintage Jaguar parked on the side of the burial service.

Chapter 22

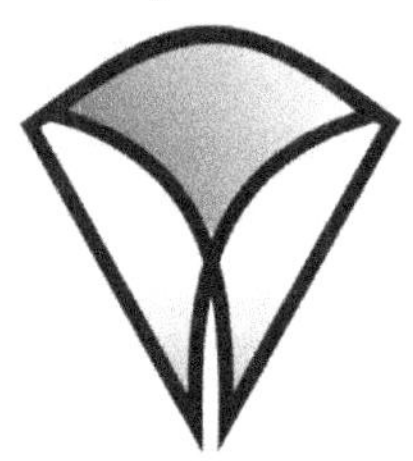

They arrived at Hotel Emma as the valet boy came to open the door. Alessandra gathered her purse and the program along with the folded-up flag as she cried behind her *Breakfast at Tiffany's* sunglasses, hugging the flag tight. She was about to step out as the door opened when Martinez, who was driving, turned and spoke in a soft, empathetic voice. She took her sunglasses off as she exposed her crying eyes.

"I'm sorry for your loss, your Highness. He was like a brother to us." Matthews turned to her from the passenger side as he exposed his mournful eyes. "He was a great friend. Great leader. And great brother. It's a loss for the entire community," he said as he nodded, whispering.

"You guys are amazing and thank you for all you have done." She put her shades back on.

"Your Highness," Martinez said in a loud whisper.

Alessandra turned as she cried again, mournfully.

"Generalissimo Romero wished love and his deepest condolences." He handed her a box and two envelopes.

She looked up in confusion as Martinez ended up nodding with a gentle smile. Alessandra smiled through her tears as she gathered the folded flag she had put down and grabbed the valet boy's hand.

As he helped her up, he softly replied, "I'm sorry for your loss Mrs. King."

She replied with a weak whimper and said in a swallowed whisper, "Thank you, Mateo."

He handed her a new room key. She looked at it in confusion as he looked at Mateo in his golden-brown eyes.

"Compliments to our beloved guest from all the hotel staff of Hotel Emma," he said in an empathetic tone.

She smiled as she cried in mourning as Mateo hugged her for a moment and excused himself while the bellhop came and gently tapped Alessandra, and she slowly turned. "Eddie will lead you to the Penthouse Suite."

Arriving at the rooftop penthouse, Eddie replied in mournful delight, "I hope you don't mind, Mrs. King. We secured all your belongings and brought them up to your room." He closed the first layer of sheer cerulean curtains. A bright light blue filter of light came through as Alessandra plopped herself robotically on the baroque brocade light in a Tiffany blue couch contrasted in a silver beige pattern. "We also have extended your stay for as long as you need. Compliments of management for the efforts you and Mr. King did to instill fairness."

She smiled and said, "Thank you, Eddie." She sat lifeless on the couch. She looked at the various arrangements of wreath sprays, bouquets, and an array of bouquets filled with white and cerulean dyed roses, white, and purple orchids, infused with dusty rose-colored roses, and peace lilies that read, “Our condolences, Alessandra.” Some wreaths said, “RIP Solider” with Jonathan’s angelic face.

Alessandra thought about the intimate night they shared in her small apartment in Houston. She remembered the last movie they shared, which evoked the song *All Out of Love* by Air Supply and how many laughs they shared watching Ryan Reynolds’ *Deadpool*.

“How weird,” Eddie looked at his phone and Alessandra as she turned to see Eddie, holding back tears.

“Thanks for the kindness, Eddie. I need some alone time,” she said in mournful sorrow.

“Yes, Mrs. King. Your meals are complimentary as well—a little special gift from the entire wait staff. The last thing you need is what to eat if you decide you rather retire in the room,” he said kindly.

“Thank you so much,” she said, now mournfully crying as Eddie came closer he opened his arms.

“May I,” Eddie asked as he hugged her while she belted out and gained control, which he quickly and gently broke the embrace as he walked toward the door. Before he shut the door, he said, “If you need anything. Just ring/” He closed the door gently behind him.

The song continued to play as she pulled the phone out of her black satin clutch and chucked the phone at the wall, which shattered the phone. Stupid fucken phone.” Her mourning turned to anger as it went silent from a short circuit.

She looked at her glow as it faded as she finally had full control of her power.

“What a fucken coincidence.” She pulled the chilled champagne bottle as the flag slapped the floor. “I’m so sorry, Babe,” she said to the flag as she held it close and hard. She kissed the folded flag and said in a soft whimper, “You will always be my person.”

She gently placed it on the lounging area table that was silver and marbled as she looked at the envelopes and the velvet aqua blue box, now looking at the rose gold and light blue metallic envelope. She opened the rose gold card that read Alessandra. She opened the envelope to find a letter in familiar writing. The writing of her Uncle Mike that read.

My Dearest Niece and Goddaughter,

I can’t express how much pain and sorrow I feel. As he was like a son to me and a faithful right hand, my heart bleeds in anguish to know that I can’t be there for you in your most significant time of need. I could only imagine that the pain you had was stronger than the one you had when I first passed away. It brings me great comfort to have consoled you during that pivotal time; it makes me sad that I couldn’t be there in your time of need. Know that we mourn Jonathan Carlos Enrique Sepulveda King with loving hearts and great honor. Mrs. Sepulveda, your mother-in-law, sends a special message as she shares the loss of her beloved son. We took the liberty to control and pay the limit in advance as she insisted; we sent you a new wardrobe in the closet of the master bedroom of the suite the staff will put you in, of course, at their own will. Please close the blackout curtains before you open the box and the letter. We will be in touch soon and know that I will always love you with all my heart. Mi Nina Princessa.

Sincerely Tio Mike

P. S. I know Jonathan is proud of you wherever he may be. We will never forget those family members, always missed, and always honorably remembered. We will be in touch soon.

Alessandra hugged the letter and put it down on the dressing table as she opened a full closet full of various garments, all with price tags and some in garment bags. She closed the blackout curtains and adjusted herself to prepare what she was about to open. She took a breath and opened the envelope. It immediately glowed, and rushed out of her hands. The song that was their last dance in that empty Houston apartment before she moved back to San Antonio projected in thin air. The happiest moment of their entire life together and what they said would be their couple dance song *I Don't Want to Live Forever* by Taylor Swift and ZAYN. Along with montages of their most cherished moments that followed the beautiful star show that looked like fireworks in the galaxy in honor of her late Jonathan, which had a soft and angelic voice.

My dear beloved daughter-in-law. It pains me for tragedy to unite us, as he was my only son. Thank you for making my dear the happiest Demi-God in the entire galaxy. Thank you for making him the man he was and the noblest soul in the Universe. Before we part, I have a special message from Jonathan Carlos Enrique Sepulveda King, our Johnny before the tragedy.

Alessandra smiled as she teared up, seeing Jonathan's face appear on the projection reaching out, and for a moment, felt the gentle touch of Jonathan as she listened to his message.

"Hey, Babe. Warrior Princess. My person." He sighed in loving adornments. "If you see this message, I am sure my ass is grass."

She laughed as she wiped the tears as she softly giggled.

"I am proud and grateful to have you as a wife. I never saw you as anything less. I will always be with you. Stay strong, and remember, I will always be with you. You're not only protected by the ring I gave you but the necklace you will find in the blue box." He sighed a peaceful and loving last sigh as he said, "I'll forever and always love you. I married a badass. You're my badass. You're my person. But you're more than that; you're my eternal soulmate. I love you, Baby. Never forget the good times." He threw her a kiss she gave back, swearing that she could feel his soft lips one more time.

She opened the box. In it, she saw something he showed her that night in Houston. His family crest with one empty spot filled with a symbol of the firebird. Alessandra recognized her shield and sword on the engraved nameplate "Sepulveda King" and below it, "Johnny & Alessandra forever."

She looked at the continuous light show in the galactic sky's projection as she cried in peaceful sorrow. Alessandra held the necklace tight to her heart as she said in a whisper, “You’ll always be my person.” she closed her eyes and shed her mournful but grateful tears.

A knock on the door that resembled the same knock she heard throughout her life interrupted the moment. She bolted to the door as she swung it open in frustration as she annoyingly said, “Guys, I told you all I needed to be alone.” She dropped the box as she stood still at the door. Now her tears subsided as the box and necklace fell from her hands.

She stood there as she looked as he said, “Hello Alessandra,” cautiously. He gently kneeled to pick up the necklace as he placed it gently in her hands and cupped her manicured hand with large, rouged hands.

She broke her silence in a very sluggish and astonished whisper, “Tio Mike, is it you?”

About the Author

Frieda López is the writer and made her debut with her first book *Journey of an Unraveled Road. She* was born and raised in San Antonio, TX. Through her professional career in customer relations and retail management, she has utilized her experience and interactions with the behavioral patterns, which was used to start her personal journey. She has completed philosophy, psychology, and theology courses at San Antonio College as well as creative writing courses. Frieda López has been a lifelong writer since 2nd grade. She works from home in San Antonio, TX.

Journey of an Unraveled Road

Available on Amazon

"Journey of an Unraveled Road" reveals the journey of a woman plagued by childhood trauma and her uncharted journey revealing a perceived reality through a distorted pair of rose glasses. Faced with life's problems, she discloses the errors of her ways that enabled a lifetime of harmful behavioral patterns, which allowed people through her journey to perform the ultimate sin. As a result, each decision she made, molded her happiness and authentic self through her stigmas, insecurities, and fears. Armed with courage and accountability, she slowly repairs the wounds of the past to silence the ghost that once haunted her transforming into a uniquely changed version revealing her true self, which begins the journey of an unraveled road she now is on.

www.ingramcontent.com/pod-product-compliance
Lightning Source LLC
LaVergne TN
LVHW051058080426
835508LV00019B/1955

* 9 7 8 1 6 4 9 5 3 0 6 9 1 *